The Last Golden Calf
The Microchip Identity

Henry W. Vandergriff

Lamb Publishing

D1214947

The Last Golden Calf
© 2002 by Henry W. Vandergriff

Printed in the USA by Sheridan Books, Inc. for,
Lamb Publishing, 11000 Leesville Road, Raleigh NC 27613

Cover Design by Senior Graphics Designer and Artist, Lant Elrod

Prayer Partners: Anthony Godley, Edith Jackson, Peter Harrison and Van Vandergriff

Research Assistant: Jesse Vandergriff

Editing Consultant: Phil Snapp

Written: August, 2001- May, 2002

See Web Page: LambPublishing.Com

ISBN: 0-9719626-0-X

Library of Congress Card Number (LCCN) Application Made

The Last Golden Calf
The Microchip Identity

Dedicated to:

My wife Linda, our six children, our congregation
and all those who have supported this ministry
by patiently listening and encouraging
me to share my heart.

Contents

Part I: The Microchip Identity's Development

The scriptures warn; loving money causes many to err from the faith and pierces men's souls with many sorrows. Money's history can be traced from cattle, to precious metals, coins, paper, plastic, and the newest form; a microchip designed to be implanted in the human hand. Could this be the prophetic "mark of the beast" spoken of two thousand years ago in Revelation?

Social architects have been developing the universal personal identification code for the purpose of identifying every human on the earth. The implanted microchip has been used for pet identification and now for human identification. This microchip is being proposed as a fraud proof system for national identification.

Although in its infancy, the infrastructure for the microchip identity is being implemented all around us. It may come as a surprise just how much you are presently using the microchip identity that is designed to replace everything in your wallet.

The microchip identity will eliminate identity fraud and open the door to a future of possibilities, revolutionizing the way people live. These benefits will seduce mankind to receive the implant even though severe spiritual consequences are attached.

Why should people resist the microchip identity? Does the chip invite government control that eliminates freedom? When the colonists wrote the Declaration of Independence, they summarized their reasons for breaking away from the despotism of King George. These reasons are parallel to the microchip identity.

Part II: The Golden Calf

History reveals ancient cultures worshipped cows in astrology, Egypt, Mesopotamia and India. Cattle were the first measurement of wealth and the cow's worship is the same rationale used when men receive the microchip identity.

When Israel rebelled, they made a golden calf and declared the image to be God. The carnality of Israel's golden calf is the same spirit today as America embraces the microchip identity.

Solomon spent his first twenty years building God's house. He spent the next twenty years accumulating women, horses, gold and silver. His double life laid the foundation for golden calf worship to be resurrected at the height of Israel's glory.

Solomon's carnality caused the kingdom to split. Israel worshipped the golden calves of Jeroboam while Judah held onto God. The history of Israel's golden calves and divided nation hold important lessons. Is America really, "One nation unto God, indivisible?"

How does one put a face on the spirit of covetousness? Three Biblical stories; Gehazi, Balaam, and the moneychangers reveal how men erred from the faith because they loved money. Their lifestyles are expressions of America's covetousness.

Part III: What Remains is More Glorious!

Pagan nations questioned God's power to lead the Hebrews through the wilderness. God demonstrated His glory and made an awesome promise to the saints living in the last days.

Preface

The week *Mystery Babylon: The Coming Microchip Economy,* came off the press in October of 2000, a Florida based company publicly announced in New York city a functioning prototype of a microchip for human implantation for e-commerce. Suddenly the media was hungry for news, and I was considered a source.

The media focus resulted in over a hundred radio and TV talk show stations doing programs on the subject. Since most were secular programs, many hosts would tell me before going on the air, "We just want to emphasize the technology, not the religious ramifications" of this microchip implant. My response was, "Are you going to take on-air phone calls?" "Of course," to which I replied, "People are going to ask about the Bible."

The media's interest quickened me to further research the microchip technology, so I could adequately answer their questions. I was amazed at what I found. *The Last Golden Calf: The Microchip Identity* is the result of my research. This book reveals the evolution of money from cattle, to coin, to paper, to plastic, and to microchip implantation with a spiritual explanation of why the advancement is happening and how Christians should respond.

Another reason is to calm people's fears. Many well meaning Christians say talking about the mark of the beast will cause those on the spiritual fence to fall away.

Jesus said, "These things I have spoken to you, that you should not be made to stumble...[for] the time is coming that whoever kills you will think that he offers God service."[1] Jesus obviously thought talking about an uncomfortable subject would help Christians mature so they *would not* stumble. Likewise, talking about the mark of the beast will bring about Christian maturity.

Having read the Scriptures on a regular basis for thirty years, I have discovered the Bible is a remarkable book. God loves mankind and shares future events that will affect the nations. He says, "Surely the Lord God does nothing, unless He reveals His secret to His servants the prophets."[2] I believe one can discern the future by prayerful consideration of these prophets. God says the events of old were written in Scripture to be like billboards along the path of life to give understanding concerning the end of the age.[3]

It is prudent to understand future events. Any Wall Street investor will pursue high yielding growth funds if the economy is bullish. However, the same investor will pull his funds into conservative bonds to weather the economy during bear markets. In the same way, men should consider God's prophetic voice and invest their faith wisely. It is foolish to ignore God's truths and to suffer spiritual consequences when God has so lovingly provided His direction for spiritual prosperity.

The threefold purpose of *The Last Golden Calf* is first, to examine the development of the microchip for identification and economic purposes, second, to discover how this microchip is like the ancient cult of the golden calf, and finally, to inspire Christians to faith and patience.

Admittedly there are many voices when it comes to end time prophecy, so much so that one becomes dull of hearing because of past disappointments. I too have been greatly disillusioned in times past with the voices of popular opinions, such as what one's favorite preacher said or what was sold in the prophecy section of the Christian bookstore. It has been my determination to listen to others articulate their perspectives with patience and then consider them in light of the Scriptures. I then hold fast to that which is good and let go of that which does not align itself with the Bible.[4]

It is paramount to spiritual development that you read God's word for your own convictions. Two thousand years ago the Apostle Paul said concerning the future, "We see in a mirror, dimly."[5] That faint image is getting clearer and clearer as we approach the end of the age. Though each of us has been frustrated with the diffused voices of the past, we should not give up pursuing God for clarity about future events. To do so is to wax dull of hearing.

Consider what our Lord said to the prophet Daniel. "Go your way, Daniel, for the words are closed up and sealed till the time of the end."[6] Note that our Lord did not say the words were sealed up forever, just until the end. The prophet Jeremiah proclaimed, "In the latter days you will understand it perfectly."[7]

"Understanding the end perfectly" is contrary to the present persuasion that says, "You do not know what hour your Lord is coming."[8] Yet the whole purpose of the book of Revelation is God's desire to show saints things, which will shortly take place before the revealing of Christ, hence the title "The Revelation."[9] The word "hour" in the Greek, pronounced ho'rah is used consistently throughout the New Testament and it means, literally or figuratively, "instant, hour, day, or season."

Jesus said we do not know the instant, hour or day. But He expects us to know the season!

Consider Jesus' admonitions to the church in Sardis, "Remember therefore how you have received and heard; hold fast and repent. Therefore if you will not watch, I will come upon you as a thief, and you will not know what hour I will come upon you."[10] In this passage, Jesus is encouraging us to walk in repentance so *we may know the hour* of His coming. Since we will not know the instant, hour or day, He must be talking about the season with really close accuracy.

Jesus challenged the Pharisees of His day saying, "When it is evening you will say, 'It will be fair weather, for the sky is red'; and in the morning, 'It will be foul weather today, for the sky is red and threatening.'... You know how to discern the face of the sky, but you cannot discern the signs of the times."[11] Jesus acknowledged their accurate assessments of the weather and chided them for not understanding the signs of the spiritual seasons. He fully expected them to know the signs of the times, just as they understood predicting weather.

Today Doppler weather forecasts can actually show through radar the approaching warm and cold fronts. Weathermen accurately predict the five-day forecasts of sun and rain along with temperatures to within a few degrees. In these last days, God is opening the Scriptures to understand the signs of the times to within a season. As the end approaches, the mirror grows brighter, and we will understand perfectly. Please read with an open heart and pursue God with a renewed vision for faith and patience.

<>< Henry W. Vandergriff

Part I

The Microchip Identity's Development

*"Why do the nations rage, and the people plot a
vain thing? The kings of the earth set themselves,
and the rulers take counsel together, against the
Lord and against His Anointed, saying, Let us
break their bonds in pieces and cast away their
cords from us. He who sits in the heavens shall
laugh; The Lord shall hold them in derision."*
Psalm 2:1-4

One

Man's Amazing Ingenuity: Money

"But those who desire to be rich fall into temptation and a snare.... For the love of money is the root of all kinds of evil, for which some have strayed from the faith...."
1 Timothy 6:9-10

An innovative form of money is being developed for the new millennium. In the near future, a hypodermic needle will inject a microchip under the skin of your right hand or forehead. The microchip is designed to carry an identification number that is exclusive to your body's physical attributes. The new identity chip will give access to a whole new world of buying and selling in the world of electronic commerce called the "theory of particle finance".

Jesus told the prophet John about this new form of monetary exchange nearly two thousand years ago.[1] He attached a severe consequence to the use of this money. John said those who received this mark in their hand or forehead would lose their opportunity for salvation and instead be tormented with fire and brimstone forever.[2]

Whenever I tell people about this ancient prophecy and the development of the microchip identity, their reactions are mixed. Some treat the subject with a "ho hum" approach as if to say, "I do not really believe it". Others smile with, "you cannot stop progress," and still others acknowledge their belief in the Scriptures and say, "it is not for me".

At this point I cannot help wondering what every man's decision will be. After all, the consequences are eternal. Some will choose to accept the microchip with no understanding of its spiritual significance. Others will be caught in the valley of decision and choose to accept the microchip so they can hold onto their current lifestyle. They will rationalize the microchip as an important step in the evolution of society and discard its eternal ramifications.

But true Christians will refuse to accept the microchip implant. They will recognize the strategy of Satan to lure men's allegiance away from God to trusting man's world system for sustenance. They will remember the biblical warnings concerning the last days and hold fast to the promise of Jesus Christ "to never leave nor forsake them".[3]

Perhaps the haunted house in Disney World can help us understand the end time scenario. Each time I visit the haunted house, I am fascinated with its spookiness. The doorman exhorts the visitors grimly, "please step into the *dead* center of the room." Immediately you realize there are no doors to this room and you are trapped with no way out! "Unless of course, you choose my way out", chides the devious voice on the overhead speaker. Suddenly, lightning strikes the darkened room and there a suicidal body hangs from the ceiling, swaying to the screams of naive patrons. A door opens and a chair on a conveyor belt transports you past haunting scenes with throbbing sinister music. The heart pounds with fear

while logic reasons "its just entertainment." Eventually
you come to the ballroom floor where ghosts appear
dancing. The spirits disappear and reappear. You literally
see right through them. They are there, the eyes are sure
of it. You are informed by a creepy voice that the ghosts
are going home with you and as the ride ends, there in the
mirror is a ghost sitting in the buggy with you. Of course
I laugh and tell my doubtful child, it is not real. We're
just having fun and the devil is not really going home
with us. My little one composes her self and shouts,
"Let's do it again!" So off we run to ride it once more.

It is not real! Of course its not! It is just fun to bring
one's fear to the surface and then subdue the frightened
soul. But these "end times" are not Disney World. Satan
longs for you to dismiss the two thousand year-old
prophecy of the mark in the right hand as coincidence. It
does not matter that man throughout history has only
bought and sold with cash or bartered until this century.

Even though the prophetic fulfillment of God's
warnings are right before men eyes, Satan persuades men
to discard the prophecy as a mirage of reality. But unlike
Disney World, once you have agreed the microchip
identity has no spiritual significance, the evil spirit really
does go home with you. The successful deceiver mocks
with laughter as you are enclosed in the darkened room
where there is no way out but spiritual suicide.

So let's take a moment to discover the origins of
money and it's progressive development throughout
history. Money is the amazing creation of human intellect
having three basic components. First, it is accepted as a
medium of exchange. Second, it is a store of value
because it exists only in limited quantities, and third,
people must have confidence or faith in it.

Ancient Money

The love of money can be seen in the ancient worship of cattle. To this day the Hindu culture honors the cow with a mystical reverence. Cow worship is rooted in the ancestral heritage of shepherding. Later generations equated the partaking of the cow's dairy products with their parents' nurturing, hence, the transference of respect that somehow the life of the parent must be co-existent with the life of the cow.

In the ancient time of Abraham, wealth was measured in "cattle"[4]. The size of one's livestock or herd was an obvious mark of prosperity. The oldest known Scriptures reflected the wealth of Job in the enormity of his herds as well.[5]

The importance of cattle as money can still be seen in our language today. The word *pecuniary*, meaning monetary, comes from the Latin word *pecus*, which means cattle. Livestock produced milk, cheese and meat for eating. The hides were fashioned into shoes, clothing, and belts. The horns became musical instruments, tools and weapons. The products were then traded to others for goods of their making.

> *The word pecuniary, meaning monetary, comes from the Latin word pecus, which means cattle.*

This old fashioned wealth exchange is called "bartering", and was the predominate mode of buying and selling until the introduction of coinage. Bartering is still used in third world countries today and was an active part of America's economy in the past century.

People living off the land did not need money for daily living; instead they bartered. This is how bartering worked in America. The rural farmer would bring a wagonload of wheat to the miller, who would grind it into flour. The farmer would leave a sack of flour as payment and drive to the general store. There he would exchange the flour for provisions of salt, beef jerky and canned goods. The farmer would exchange flour with the blacksmith for sharpening the plow and the gunsmith for ammunition. Payment could have been made with coins or gold certificates, but it was not necessary. The price of flour was printed in the newspaper everyday and everyone understood its value.

Coinage

Silver and gold as a medium of exchange was transferred by weight. That weight could take the form of jewelry[6] or objects of daily use. Gold might be carried by weight as a wedge or thin bar found by Achan at Jericho.[7] The precious metals were also carried as dust or fragments that could easily be melted down for immediate purposes.

"The oldest known coins were struck during the ancient kingdom of Lydia in the seventh century B.C. The tiny thumbnail-size lumps bore the royal emblem of a lion's head. Merchants, long accustomed to settling accounts in precious metals, must have found them useful; by using coins, they did not have to do as much weighing for each transaction. By the fourth century B.C. a weight unit called the shekel, used by ancient Babylonians, Phoenicians, and Israelites, had lent its name to silver coins. Many of today's currencies, the Italian lira, the British pound, the peso and peseta of Spanish-speaking countries, are named for units of weight once used to measure amounts of metal, mostly silver."[8]

The striking of coins by government was an attempt to guarantee the weight and purity of the precious metal.

The spread of coinage to Judah seems to have been slow, because of the images they bore. Early Jewish coins heeded the second of the Ten Commandments, "Thou shalt not make unto thee any graven image".[9] Their coinage adhered strictly to horticultural designs and inanimate objects. Coins minted under Herod breached the law as they displayed the reigning emperor's head.[10] This taboo stuck at the heart of Jewish worship: "You shall not bow down to them nor serve them. For I, the Lord your God, am a jealous God..."[11] Hence the outrage of Jewish zealots against Herod, who was appointed by Caesar of Rome and therefore an extension of the Roman government.

However, examination of the commandment reveals the stamping of coins with images of agriculture would equally breach the law. The command says, "You shall not make for yourself a carved image-any likeness of *anything* that is in heaven above or that is in the earth beneath, or that is under the earth."[12] The Bible says, "God is Spirit, and those who worship Him must worship in spirit and truth."[13] The true spirit of worship trusts the God who made the earth to bring forth wheat, not the wheat itself.

Miscellaneous Forms

Throughout history, money has taken many primitive forms such as stones and shells. American Indians used tiny clamshells called wampum. The shells were drilled and threaded for necklace attire.

African tribes have used pigs, blocks of salt and even slaves as dowry in exchange for a wife. The International

Primitive Money Society displays Fiji bowls and Malaysian drums that have been used as mediums of exchange. The fact is money can be any medium people agree upon and are willing to trust.

Paper Money

"The earliest paper currency issued by a government appeared in China in the 11th century.   In Persia the Mongol ruler Geikhatu decreed paper money in 1294 A.D., but merchants refused to accept it. They closed their shops and hid their goods. Trade stopped. Facing revolt, Geikhatu rescinded his edict; the official who suggested it in the first place was torn to pieces in the bazaar." [14] Paper money did not appear again until 1661. European bank notes were printed in Sweden when coins were in short supply. Paper money had a turbulent beginning, yet today paper money is universally trusted as a medium of exchange.

America developed trust in paper money by backing their certificates with silver and gold. Green dollar bills with yellow backs could be taken to any bank and exchanged for silver or gold coins.

> *Paper money first appeared in the 11th century. The man who suggested it was torn to pieces in the Bazaar. Today, paper money is universally trusted.*

In the mid-nineteen-forties, an exhibit of bank notes in Washington D.C. explained the gold standard. The dollar bill was said to be worth one thirty-fifth of a troy ounce of gold. The exhibit displayed the currencies of foreign nations with the corresponding value written underneath their paper money. Foreign governments could exchange American money for gold at the U.S. Treasury. However, foreign demand for gold became so rampant that the gold exchange was suspended in 1971.

Finally, the gold standard was abandoned in 1978. As a result, international currencies float in value, reflecting supply and demand. Foreign currency values are a reflection of trust. A government can abuse the people's trust by simply printing more money, thus creating an over supply, which cheapens the currency and causes the citizens to look for safer money.

As an American, I have rarely been to a third world country that its citizens did not covet my American dollars over their own paper bills. Businesses and individuals gladly exchange goods and services, for the American dollar's stability is a hedge against inflation within their own country. If the foreigner's money inflates, my U.S. dollar is worth the inflated value of the cheapened money. Thus allowing him to save with confidence, whereas the domestic currency is forcing him to spend quickly, as it buys less and less with each new day.

Peru is an example of this abuse. In 1986, the "sol" (Spanish for sun) was being exchanged at 14,000 to one U.S. dollar. So the government issued a new currency called the "inti" (Quechuan for sun) and began exchanging them at 14 to the dollar. People quickly discerned the switch. Within five years, a soda was selling for 500,000 intis. The unrestrained government issued new money and changed the name back to the "sol". The "sol-inti-sol" currency inflated 2,200,000 percent over the course of several years.

The Hungarian "pengo" is the worst example of inflation. When the nation discovered its gold reserves were stolen by Germany during World War II, inflation took off like the space shuttle. The "pengo" was eventually expressed in notes of a million, million billion. That number is written with a one followed by 21 zeros. Within months the government restored confidence by issuing new paper money called the "forint" with gold backing.

"The Nightly Business Report" gives the fluctuating value of foreign currencies against the dollar at the end of each day. The foreign exchange rate is a reflection of the trust banking institutions have of other currencies based on that nation's economic policies.

So how far have Americans come in trusting our own government's paper money? In Washington D.C. and Fort Worth, Texas, the U.S. Treasury Department's Bureau of Engraving and Printing prints paper money. It is 75 percent cotton and 25 percent linen. The dollar last an average of eighteen months before it is worn out. Turned in by a bank, the dollar will be destroyed by shedding and replaced. At any point in time, there are trillions of dollars in paper money being circulated by the Federal Government and in any given month, the Fed adds a few billion here or there to the circulation. This is how the increase happens.

Everyday, the Federal Open Market Committee in Washington D.C. authorizes the Federal Reserve Bank of New York to buy or sell U.S. securities and treasury bills. The promissory notes are exchanged with major banks and brokerage houses, which in turn trade them with the public. The country's money supply is increased when the Federal government pays for example, a billion dollars to security dealers for selling those notes. The dealers are credited with deposits in their banks. But where does the money come from?

The Federal Reserve creates it. According to government officials, the authority is derived from the

Federal Reserve Act of 1913, and based on the Constitution, Article I, Section 8, "Congress shall have the power...to coin money, [and] regulate the value thereof...." Thus, the Federal Reserve Central Bank has the ability to write checks, creating money that did not exist before. The checks are backed by the taxation of responsible citizens to pay the government's debts. The only limit is the people's trust in the Federal Reserve to act responsibly.

"Now watch how the Fed-created money lets our commercial banking system create even more. The Fed requires banks to put aside a portion of their depositors' funds as reserves. Say this reserve ratio is set at 10 percent. Then for every $1000.00 in new deposits, a bank must keep at least $100.00 in reserve but can loan out the rest, which is $900.00. On the bank's books this loan remains as an asset, earning interest until it is paid off. The customer who got the loan is likely to spend it right away, say for a used car. The dealer deposits the $900.00 check in his bank, which then has an additional $900.00 in reserves and can in turn loan 90 percent of that, which is $810.00. And so on and on, until the original $1000.00 put into one bank may enable dozens of banks to issue a total of $9,000.00 in new loans. Thus a hundred million dollars injected by the Fed into the commercial banking system could theoretically stimulate the appearance of 900 million dollars in new check book money, money that did not exist before. And it is all built on the assumption that the system is sound." [15]

Since this money is not backed with gold, how did the Federal Reserve develop such trust? "The Federal Reserve System was established by Congress in 1913 and began operating in 1914. Previously, many banks had failed in financial panics or business depressions. One major purpose of the Federal Reserve System was to make it possible for banks to borrow money temporarily to meet "runs" or sudden large demands by their depositors."[16] As time passed, people began to have confidence their money would "be there" in times of crisis. Thus, people began to relax about the security of their life's savings.

America's Development of Paper Money

People's faith in the system is profound. It defies logic. The Constitution, Article I Section 8 written in 1787 says, "To coin money, regulate the value thereof, and of foreign coin, and fix the standard weights and measures".[17] The founding fathers wrote this article with a harsh experience fresh in their minds. In 1775, the Second Continental Congress issued paper money. This was the first national paper money issued jointly by the Thirteen Colonies. The Continental currency was issued during the Revolutionary War and quickly lost its value as more and more was printed without the backing of gold or silver.[18] People began to say of any worthless thing, "It's not worth a Continental."

Our founding fathers understood the need to back coinage with "weights and measures" of precious metals. As a result, in 1792 Congress provided the first monetary system of the United States. It was a dual system of gold and silver. The gold dollar contained 24.75 grains of pure gold. The silver dollar contained 371.25 grains of pure silver.[19] In fact, the constitution prohibited in Article I, Section 10 (1) that, "No State shall...coin money; emit bills of credit; [or] make anything but gold and silver coin a tender in payment of debts..." to insure stability.

Nearly seventy years later, the United States Government issued its first paper money in 1861. The notes were called "demand notes" meaning, if you insisted on gold or silver, the bank would exchange the note for you. Within fifteen years four more kinds of paper currency were added. These were gold certificates, United States notes, national bank notes and silver certiciates.[20]

A law enacted by Congress in 1900 declared that the dollar "shall be the standard unit of value," and shall consist of 25.8 grains of gold nine-tenths fine. The law called 'The Gold Standard Act' also directed the Secretary of the Treasury to keep all forms of money issued or coined by the United States at parity of value (that is, equality of purchasing power) with this standard. The act further stated that nothing shall affect the legal-tender quality of the silver dollar or any other money coined or issued by the United States. The Federal Reserve Act of December of 1913 again affirmed the equality provision of The Gold Standard Act of 1900.[21] When Congress abandoned the Gold Standard Act in 1978, it violated its own laws.

The founding fathers would be amazed to see people trusting coins and paper that no longer have the corresponding weight of precious metal to back their value. They did not trust the "Continental" during the Revolutionary War. Yet strangely, their faith is solid in the system today.

In the mid-nineteen-sixties, my father owned a coin-operated laundry. Each Sunday morning, he would gather all the coins from the machines. Then we sat at the kitchen table counting the money and separating the silver coins from the copper alloy coins to be put in a safety deposit box. My father was sure the country was about to suffer a major financial crisis from the devaluing of its currency, but it never happened.

Congress devalued the money as a trial balloon, to see what the response of America would be. If the citizens revolted, they could always restore the silver. If they accepted it, Congress would be ready to take the next step of abandoning the Gold Standard.

The slogan printed on American money is, "In God We Trust." There is certainly no precious metal girding the paper money up. So is it God, or another reason for the soundness of our monetary system?

The Federal Reserve System was created to help establish money and banking conditions that would make the country prosperous. Their main job was to keep the supply of paper money and bank checking deposits at levels best suited for the country's economic growth.[22] America has certainly enjoyed prosperous times since the abandonment of the Gold Standard and for this we must applaud them. History proves man's creation of money requires the confidence of people and the Federal Reserve has gained America's trust. Congress discerned in 1978 that its citizens were ready to begin trusting their monetary system. It may be smoke and mirrors, but Americans are placing their faith in it.

Perhaps the god in our slogan, "In God We Trust" is more realistically referring to the god of money. Perhaps a better slogan would be, "In Man We Trust." Each time the government creates money by issuing more promissory notes, they are in affect saying, "We believe the American people will allow us to tax them to pay for these obligations." More government, more programs, more bureaucracy built on the foundation of man's trust in the system.

Credit's Development

Italian ingenuity gave a boost to the European economy in the Middle Ages. The merchants of Tuscany, began to use the bill of exchange in the 13th century to skirt around the church's ban on the lending of money with interest. The bill of exchange became the key to modern banking.

Michele Cassandro, professor of modern economic history at the University of Siena, explains how it worked: "It would say, for example, 'signor A, having received so many Sienese scudi, will pay to Signor B so many Florintine florins at such and such a place on such and such at date.' That looks like a currency exchange transaction, but in fact it is a loan agreement, with the interest hidden in the amount of florins Signor A will be paying. But it doesn't say loan, it doesn't mention interest-so, no usury!"[23]

Today, bank loans come in all kinds of "creative financing." Their abuse by the borrower is a truth known by the church from ancient times; "The rich rules over the poor, And the borrower is servant to the lender."[24]

Credit Cards

Credit cards began to appear in America in the early nineteen-fifties. Their popularity quickly spread to the rest of the world. Plastic money has a typical interest rate of 18 percent that will double your debt every four years when the balance is left unpaid.

Centuries have passed since the church influenced the conscience of men concerning the charging of interest. Today, banking institutions are ruthless in their pursuit of people to whom they can loan money. Each day offers arrive in the mail saying, "You are already approved!" The temptation of easy money snares the gullible and threatens to destroy the borrower's name if he defaults in paying.

So why do we tolerate credit cards? Because of their incredible convenience! While traveling to Europe, I found myself at a restaurant in Italy. The owner insisted that I pay him cash for the dinner I had just eaten. Since it was evening and the banks were closed, he ushered me to an ATM machine where I inserted my credit card. The machine immediately recognized me by name. I had to marvel that a machine halfway around the world could flash my name onto its screen with such monetary respect. I felt important. I receive my Italian Lira and promptly paid the restaurateur, rejoicing to be on my way without doing the dishes. Here's how my plastic money bailed me out.

The ATM's Italian computer did not recognize my card, so my request went to the CIRRUS detection system in Luxembourg, which takes note that the card was not issued in Europe. The digital signal corresponds with the detection system in New York, which discerns the card was issued in Raleigh, NC. The request confirms my bank credit and signals the okay back to New York, to Luxembourg and on to Italy. My patience is rewarded in just over ten seconds with the ATM spitting out the Italian Lira. This wizardry of wired continents is the amazing invention of the credit card. Its convenience is overwhelming and people love it.

Microchips

French inventor Roland Moreno first developed the smart card in 1974. Its popularity in Europe has risen to

an astounding 200 million in circulation. In France, every
Visa debit card has an imbedded chip. Admittedly, they
have been slow to be embraced by the American public
for a number of reasons. They are accompanied by few
financial incentives and commercial retailers are reluctant
to acquire new reader cards to replace the magnetic strip
machines. However, those hurdles will eventually be
overcome.

Today, credit institutions are hounding us to get the
new plastic "Smart Cards." Others in the industry are
called "Blue Cards" or "Mondex Cards." These plastic
cards have a microchip imbedded in them and are
predicted to be the wave of the future. According to
Henry Mundt, MasterCard's executive vice president for
global access: "The chip that we are putting on the card
now will form the platform for the ultimate in remote
access for consumers to their funds, anytime, anywhere."[25]

> *In the not too distant future, you will store money on a chip implanted under your skin*

How long will it be till the credit
card companies ask the consumers to
carry the microchip in their right
hand or forehead? Will they even
consider such an idea? You bet!

After interviewing Hugh McColl, CEO of
NationsBank, Joshua Cooper Ramo communicated in an
article for Time magazine, with a banner headline, "The
Future of Money", that in the not too distant future, you
will store money on a chip implanted under your skin.[26]
MONDEX Philippines, Inc., producer of the "Mondex
Card", uses its website to promote cash in the future. The
convenience of cash is displayed in a picture as a
microchip on the forehead of a man.[27]

God and Prophecy

The prophet Isaiah said the ability to show things in the future is the proof of God.[28] Throughout the Scriptures God uses prophets to foretell the future. When those events come to pass, you can rest assured that God is orchestrating those events for His purposes.

God has forewarned that before the return of Jesus Christ, men will "Receive a mark on their right hand or foreheads, and that no one may buy or sell except one who has the mark."[29] The eternal consequences associated with accepting the mark are proclaimed by the prophet John, "He shall be tormented with fire and brimstone...and the smoke of their torment ascends forever and ever; and they have no rest day or night, who ...receives the mark."[30]

Summary

As the world's system comes to its zenith, God is bringing mankind to a place of decision. Man must choose to "live by faith", refusing to join the future monetary system or "place faith" in the microchip economy and loose one's opportunity for salvation. What decision will you make? Will you walk in unbelief and allow Satan to lead you to spiritual suicide? Or, will you trust in God?

Both God and the world's system are offering to be your source of sustenance. Remember Jesus said, "What will it profit a man if he gains the whole world, and loses his own soul?"[31] The entire chapter of Revelation eighteen speaks of a financial system that collapses under the judgment of God. The merchants of that system are said to have the ability to buy the "bodies and souls of men"[32], and deceive the nations of the world. Which decision will you make?

In part two, we will discover man's faith in this technological wizardry is the same faith expressed in an ancient cult of the golden calf. In the next chapter, we will examine the formation of this future monetary system and why men will soon be clamoring to receive the implanted microchip identity.

Two

The Microchip Identity's Evolution

*"He causes all, both small and great, rich and poor to
receive a mark on their right hand or foreheads, and that
no one may buy or sell except one who has the mark of
the beast...." Revelation 13:16-17*

As a college student in the early 1970's, I found
myself pondering the above Scripture as the marketing
professor began to explain the coming universal product
code (UPC). He instructed, "These black bars will appear
on every product known to man and will be scanned by
point of purchase machines worldwide to alleviate long
lines at the check out counter." Strange I thought, men
will actually buy and sell and a mark will be a part of
every transaction.

During a recent visit to the third world country of
Bolivia, my hosts excitedly drove me to their brand new
grocery store. High in the Andes Mountains, there were
aisles of shelves laden with products bearing the black
bar code. As we checked out, I could not help but marvel
as the Quechuan Indian cashier whisked the product
across the eye of the laser to read the pertinent
information regarding my purchase.

Some fifty years earlier, a man named Joseph Woodland[1] was asked to pioneer this UPC system for IBM. I had the privilege of speaking with Mr. Woodland in 1992, just after he was awarded the National Medal of Technology by then President George Bush. I asked him about the possibility of these marks being placed on human beings for identification to be used in buying and selling. Mr. Woodland informed me that I was only the second person to ever question him about the technology with regards to biblical prophecy. He dismissed my concerns and said the bars would never be used on humans.

"The universal personal identification code is designed to identify every man, woman and child on the planet."

"What do you see in the future, that will be used in men's right hand or forehead?" I asked. He then began to explain a technology called the "universal personal identification code" (UPIC). The technology is design to identify every man, woman and child on the planet, he enlightened.

According to Mr. Woodland, there are three ways a person is uniquely different from other humans. First, the iris of the eye is like a snowflake, which is diverse from all others. Second are fingerprints and third are the vocal chords. Each of these human attributes has security technologies designed around them. Another has been introduced with the discovery of human DNA and is presently being developed. Lastly, Mr. Woodland made clear that microchips could be inserted beneath the skin in conjunction with these biological features.

The UPIC can be designed around any of these unique human qualities that are given to each individual by God. A numeric value can be given to any of the body's unique physical expressions, iris, fingerprints, vocal chords or DNA and then etched onto a microchip for insertion into the right hand or forehead. For example, one possibility is the numerical expression for the contours of an individual's iris. Thus the microchip puts forth a fraud proof identification when the numeric value of the individual's iris is matched to the number etched within the microchip.[2] These human attributes are referred to as "biometric identifiers."

It is interesting to note, the abbreviation for the universal personal identification code is prophetic. UPIC is a billboard for spiritual insight when interpreted in light of its eternal consequences of hell, "you pick, you choose!" God forewarned long ago, "My people are destroyed for a lack of knowledge."[3]

> *The abbreviation for the universal personal identification code is prophetic. UPIC is a billboard for spiritual insight when interpreted in light of its eternal consequences of hell, "you pick, you choose!"*

Pet Identification

Animal shelters began developing a way to identify pets in the late 1970's. Mike Beigel invented a biochip for American Veterinary Identification Devices in California, to communicate information. This microchip started a whole new industry devoted to identifying pets, horses, cattle and now, people.

Today, most animal shelters will chip your pet via a needle. A scanner reads the chip's information onto a computer screen, revealing the pet's name, address and phone number of the owner. Should the pet ever be lost and then found, the owner is contacted through a joint database maintained by many organizations like the American Kennel Club.

"Implantable microchips were tested in 1987 when International InfoPet Systems, based in Agura Hills, California, started marketing a microchip made by Destron IDI. In 1991 InfoPet changed hands and became InfoPet Identification Systems, which markets a microchip developed by Trovan, a German-based subsidiary of AEG-telefunken, which is a major supplier of this technology in Europe. During this same time, Texas Instruments got into the growing market with its TIRIS Division of Dallas, Texas. By 1993, the implantable ID market had become a mosaic of technology. Various animal shelters, clinics, and humane societies began calling for a unified standardized biochip system." [4]

When the pet industry began calling for microchip implants that could be read by any scanner, manufactures began working towards compatibility. In 1991, Los Angeles became the first major city in America to implement the radio frequency identification device (RFID). For an explanation of how the radio frequency identification technology (RFID) works, see the appendix. Ever since, clever entrepreneurs have rapidly proposed ideas for biochip implants. The next frontier was human implantation.

Human Microchip Implants

In the movie, *"Mission Impossible II"*, the lead actress received a microchip implant to allow conspirators to globally track her. Does this sound sci-fi? It's not! Applied Digital Solutions (ADS) merged with Destron Fearing Corporation (a leader in the pet identification industry) to produce a microchip for human implantation called Digital Angel. The chip was unveiled and demonstrated on October 30th, 2000 in New York City.

According to CEO Richard Sullivan, the chip is powered solely by body heat and relays a signal to a ground station from the Global Positioning Satellites (GPS). The folks manning the ground station can use the signal for identifying, tracking and monitoring you. Mr. Sullivan said, "make no mistake about it, implantation is on the way."[5]

The benefits of the microchip are numerous. They include being able to monitor the health of chronically ill patients with ailments such as Alzheimers, to tracking people who are at risk for kidnapping, and even throwing away your credit cards.

> *CEO Richard Sullivan said, "Make no mistake about it, implantation is on the way."*

ADS stated their plans to market the device for a number of uses, including a "tamper proof means of identification for enhanced e-business security."[6] CEO Richard Sullivan said, "Although we're in the early developmental phase, we expect to come forward with applications in many different areas, from medical monitoring to law enforcement. However, in keeping with our core strengths in the e-business to business arena, we plan to focus our initial development efforts on the growing field of e-commerce security and user ID verification."[7]

The "e" in e-commerce stands for "electronic". According to Steve Cone, an executive with Fidelity Investments, "Between 40% and 50% of financial transactions today use cash and checks."[8] That means 50-60% of all financial transactions are electronic. People are slowly giving in to the idea of going to a cashless society. Each time you use a credit or debit card, electronic money is transferred. Ultimately, the microchip implanted in your hand will be scanned, and money will be electronically transferred from your account instead of using plastic cards.

"A few years ago there may have been resistance, but not anymore, people are getting used to having implants. New century, new trend. We will be a hybrid of electronic intelligence and our own soul. There is no connection to the Bible."

According to Dr. Peter Zhou, chief scientist for development of the microchip implant Digital Angel, "Demand for the implant has been tremendous, we have received requests daily from around the world for the product. One inquirer was the U.S. Department of Defense." Zhou refutes the objections of Christians, saying, "A few years ago there may have been resistance, but not anymore, people are getting used to having implants. New century, new trend." He goes on to say, "The purpose of the device is to save your life. There is no connection to the Bible."[9]

Dr. Zhou says, "Fifty years from now this will be very, very popular. Fifty years ago the thought of a cell phone, where you could walk around talking on the phone, was unimaginable. Now they are everywhere." Just like the cell phone, Digital Angel "will be a connection from yourself to the electronic world. It will be your guardian, protector. It will bring good things to you. We will be a hybrid of electronic intelligence and our own soul."[10] Gee whiz, it sounds like this microchip is being promoted with the attributes of God.

Digital Angel's parent company, ADS received a special "Technology Pioneers" award from the World

Economic Forum for it contributions to "worldwide economic development and social progress through technology advancements." The World Economic Forum, incorporated in 1971 with headquarters in Geneva, is an independent, not-for-profit organization "committed to improving the state of the world."[11]

9-11 The National ID

In the aftermath of the terrorist bombing of the World Trade Center in New York, Americans suddenly became very receptive to the idea of exchanging civil liberties for greater security. "A recent poll by the Pew Research Center showed that 2/3 of Americans support the mandatory display of a national ID card on demand in order to 'feel safe and secure.'"[12] Ideas that previously seemed un-American are now being discussed with patriotic fervor. Those discussions are centered on implementing the national ID with the very latest microchip technology.

Even Andy Rooney on the CBS News magazine, *60 Minutes* said, "We need some system for permanently identifying safe people...something better than one of these photo IDs...I wouldn't mind having something planted permanently in my arm that would identify me."[13]

> *"We need some system for permanently identifying safe people. I wouldn't mind having something planted permanently in my arm that would identify me."*
> *-Andy Rooney*

The government is searching for a fraud proof system because fourteen of the nineteen terrorists involved in the 9-11 attacks had forged ID papers. The Washington Post reported this news story, "State motor vehicle authorities are working on a plan to create a national identification system for individuals that would link all driver databases and employ high-tech cards with a fingerprint, *computer chip* or other unique identifier."[14]

> *"Implantation makes it a 'tamper-proof' means of identification, 'substantially diminishing theft, loss, duplication or counterfeit.'"*

An old Chinese proverb says, "The symbol for the words *crises* and *opportunity* are much the same." The World Trade Center tragedy surfaced an opportunity for security-identification companies to offer solutions to the government. ADS with their implantible microchip called, "VeriChip" just happened to be positioned to seize the moment.

In an article titled, "Your Papers Please...", World Net Daily's Sherrie Gossett writes, "The VeriChip is a syringe-injectable radio-frequency device about the size of the tip of a ballpoint pen. It's designed to carry a unique ID number and other critical personal data. Once injected, the chip can be activated by an external scanner, and radio frequency signals then transmit the ID number and other stored information to an... FDA-compliant data-storage site."[15] Sherrie quotes ADS officials, "implantation makes it a 'tamper-proof' means of identification, 'substantially diminishing theft, loss, duplication or counterfeit.'"[16]

The national microchip ID was being considered long before the 9-11 crisis as evidenced by the relationship between Secretary of Commerce Norman Mineta (under then President Clinton) and ADS. Secretary Mineta was a keynote speaker on several occasions for ADS. At one such event, CEO Richard Sullivan introduced the Secretary by saying, "Secretary Mineta has been a champion of 'digital inclusion' [microchip implantation]...He has been an advocate of creating viable partnerships between the public and private sectors as part of a national digital inclusion campaign...I just want to say how delighted we are at Applied Digital Solutions to launch an exciting new partnership with you and the federal government in the important area of digital inclusion", to which Mineta replied, "I applaud you, Dick Sullivan, for your success and the direction you are taking with Applied Digital Solutions...As a nation, we cannot afford to miss out on this technology."[17]

Norman Mineta emerged as the Secretary of Transportation under President Bush. He carried his enthusiasm for microchip identification into his new role of developing a National Identification Card with State driver licenses.

> *"As a nation, we cannot afford to miss out on this technology."*
> *-Norman Mineta*
> *U.S. Secretary of Commerce*

It remains to be seen as to which microchip-identification technology emerges with the nation's approval. But the microchip is being trumpeted for its advancement over the present fraud riddled system. "'Are we going to see chips embedded in the human body? You bet we are,' said Paul Saffo, a director of The Institute for the Future (Menlo Park, Calif.). 'But it isn't going to happen overnight'... Eventual adoption analysts expressed confidence that the concept would eventually be adopted but were skeptical about its immediate future. 'For this to work, you are going to need a standard that everyone agrees to,' said Saffo...."[18]

First Americans With Biochip Implants

According to ADS, the Food and Drug Administration (FDA) approved the "VeriChip" for human implantation on April 4, 2002.[19] In the following month on May 10th , the Jacobs became the first American family to receive the microchip implant for the purpose of identification. The surgical implantation was part of ADS' national rollout campaign called "Get Chipped." [20] The procedure took less than 30 seconds and was carried live on national television's "Today Show." Jeffrey, Leslie and son Derek marveled to NBC's Katie Couric, at how simple and easy the surgical implantation was.

The Mark of the Beast?

Many companies have been working on microchips for human implantation over the past several decades. ADS was the first to acknowledge their intentions for the purpose of human identification with implantation.

> *"The wording was exactly the same as that used under the Destron Fearing animal tracking page, with the substitution of 'indivdiual' for 'animal.'" This gives new meaning to the phrase, "mark of the beast."*

According to a company website, "the method of implantation was said to be 'similar to a routine vaccination' and contain the '*individual's* unique ID number' which would be 'stored permanently, just under the skin, where it cannot be lost or altered.' The microchip was said to remain for 'the life of the *individual* with the unique ID number intact.' The wording was exactly the same as that used under the Destron Fearing *animal* tracking page, with the substitution of '*individual*' for '*animal*.'" [21]

This certainly gives new meaning to the phrase, the "mark of the beast." The Jacobs family is ironically named after Jacob, the father of Israel who was one of the three patriarchs of faith in the Bible: Abraham, Isaac and Jacob. Like the children of Israel who departed from God to worship the golden calf, the Jacobs have chosen the "mark of the beast."

Summary

Man's suspicions and fears are slowly being eroded away. Money is the creation of man and each progression of money's evolution is an incremental step forward in the trust of man's ingenuity. Amazingly, that trust is bringing mankind to a place of allowing a microchip to be implanted into the hand or forehead, contrary to the will of God.

Man's lust for security, wealth, and access to the world of materialism is spiritual confusion. Is man's identity in the image of God or in government? And if one can put trust in man's system, why can't he put trust in God? Why must one blindly follow the plan of Satan, which robs the individual of personal salvation? Trusting an individual, system or government is an expression of faith. So why not trust God who saves?

The Psalmist said, "A prudent man foresees evil and hides himself, but the simple pass on and are punished."[22] Those who desire to be Godly will consider the present technology and protect themselves from being deluded into receiving the microchip implant. In the next chapter, we will examine how the infrastructure of the microchip economy is already being implemented all around us. Its usage everyday is building trust in the system and luring mankind into the demonic plan of receiving the microchip identity.

Three

The Microchip Economy is Here!

"In the last days perilous times will come: For men will be lovers of themselves, lovers of money...without self control...lovers of pleasure rather than lovers of God."
2 Timothy 3:1-4

A safari hunter used a technique for snaring lions to be sold to the circus. The trapper would dig a large pit, place boards over the hole with camouflage and place raw meat on the center of the trap. The drifting aroma of the salted meat would draw the lion to the delicious food. Once there, he enjoyed the delightful meal before settling down for a long nap. The patient hunter would repeat the process each week, laying one less board over the pit.

The lion had plenty of food available in the field, but the convenience of the free lunch was overwhelming. There was no waiting for the prey, no struggle in the kill, no breaking of bones or gnashing of teeth. Plus, the lion could stretch his evening rest.

The lion's majesty was slowly being snared. His thunderous roar was soon missing from the silent night, the stealth in his stalk was sluggish, and his quickness and pounce, pining. Soon after falling through the camouflaged pit, his freedom was confined to the iron bars of a circus cage. The king of the jungle was now a slave for the entertainment of those who would ponder his former greatness.

Technology's Convenience

In large communities with toll roads, city planners have incorporated the RFID (Radio Frequency Identification Device) microchip to alleviate waiting to pay your toll. This is the same technology being used in microchips about the size of a grain of rice that is being inserted into our pets. In New York it's called "Easy Pass", in Los Angeles the "Fast Pass" and in Orlando the "E-Pass" system. The "E" stands for electronic. Approaching the toll station, you no longer need to stop and chuck in a quarter, the microchip communicates your account information with the toll booth and automatically deducts the payment.

One New Yorker who is a conscientious objector to the idea said, "originally they had one lane for the cars with microchips, then two, then more were added on the eight lane highway. Now they only have one lane for those who refuse this microchip 'Easy Pass' and we have to wait in line forever to get through the toll." The subtle message is: if you want convenience, take the chip.

"Today's Way to Pay"

Mobil and Exxon oil has been aggressively advertising their "Speed Pass" to attract customers. Customers sign up and get a small key chain that has a microchip. Instead of inserting your credit card at the gas pump, or going inside to pay, you simply wave the "Speed Pass" key chain by the unit's signal device and immediately you're pumping gas. Your identity is acknowledged and payment is deducted. Notice their slogan, "Today's Way To Pay." The only difference between this Speed Pass and the mark of the beast mentioned in Revelation is a thin layer of skin.

Perhaps you have seen the IBM TV ads proclaiming the future convenience of the cell phone. The ad shows a man walking up to a vending machine and punching a code on his phone. Instantly the soft drink rolls out, no cash, no credit card, just an electronic deduction on his wealth account that will appear on the month's ending statement.

> *Notice their slogan, "Today's Way to Pay." The only difference between the Speed Pass and the "mark of the beast" is a thin layer of skin.*

Another TV ad promoting future store convenience shows a man gathering his desired items. As he walks out of the store, a voice comes on above the sliding doors and says, "Thank you Mr. Smith for your business", acknowledging his purchase. The idea is to sell the customer convenience. Store management doesn't want him to wait in line. After all, time is money. How does the technology work? It's the same principle as the little gadget tagged on expensive products that sets off an alarm if you try to leave without paying for it. Business leaders are simply taking the technology to the next level. The product's microchip price tag communicates with the register your chosen goods, marks on the sales tax and deducts the amount from your microchip identity account.

The Wallet Card

"MasterCard has invested millions in the development of an E-cash system called Mondex. Smart Mondex cards have tiny embedded microchips that can store not only electronic dollars but also five other types of currency."[1] American Express calls their card the "Blue" and Visa's is called the "Smart Card." This card is so versatile, it is referred to as a "wallet card" at Mondex's website, for its ability to replace everything in your wallet.

Consider your wallet's contents. The chip's memory replaces all your magnetic strip cards with its ability to deduct from multiple accounts. The smart card becomes your ATM card or debit card. The microchip can even contain a picture of you and become your driver's license ID. The same chip can be used to access your insurance information; replace your social security card, voter registration card and library card.[2]

Mondex Philippines, Inc. recently announced a contract with China to issue a national identification card to its 1.2 billion citizens. This nation alone represents 20% of the earth's population. This means every citizen will be getting a plastic card with a microchip imbedded in it. The Chinese's identity will soon be in the microchip. Will social architects be content with people having a plastic card with a microchip for identification?

The Chinese's identity will soon be in a microchip. That is 20% of the earth's population.

As mentioned earlier, Mondex Philippines advertised on their website a picture of a man with a microchip on his forehead with a banner headline that reads, "Cash in the Future." The ultimate plan of social architects is to implant the chip under your skin.

The Digital Economy

Wachovia Bank used TV ads to urge consumers to join the "digital economy." They did this by offering a plastic "Smart Card" with an imbedded microchip. The 30-second ad showed the joy of convenience brilliantly displayed on the smiling faces of those obtaining the card. Digital economy, what is that? The future of money is tied to the theory of particle finance in cyber space. The next generation is expected to learn how to use on-line banking via personal computers.

My teenage son went to the bank to open a checking account. The deal he got for free checking was interesting. He had to make all deposits and withdrawals from the ATM and if he came inside the bank to see a teller, it would cost him eight dollars per visit. Yikes! That's a lot of money to a teenager. It's also a powerful incentive to break the behavioral habits of his parents' generation.

Banks are scrambling to keep up with changing technology and increase profit. They do this by cutting costs. They save money by eliminating the need for tellers. Less tellers reduces paperwork, salaries, medical benefits and overhead. The chip cards help eliminate $1.09 billion that credit card companies lose to fraud annually, according to the Nilson Report, an industry newsletter.[3] The chip cards are much more durable than the magnetic strip cards and reduce the hassle and expense of replacement. By convincing customers to do business with a microchip, instead of cash or check, the record keeping is done by computer software, not by human hands.

Recently I opened my cell phone to make an adjustment. I could not help but notice the SIM card inside. SIM stands for subscriber identity module. My identity is the microchip in the phone. This small microchip on a piece of punched out plastic (same as a smart card) fits into a slot next to the circuitry of the mobile phone.

Merely pressing the power button on the mobile phone triggers a million lines of computer code.[4] The phone bill alone is amazing. It spells out each phone number called, the length of the call, whether outgoing or incoming and tallies the minutes to figure my bill. All this information was processed through the air to signal towers and deducted from my credit card at the end of each month. No mail, no check to write and no stamp to lick.

The Future of Money

The future of money is changing over from paper and plastic to one of electronic digits on a computer screen. "William Niskanen, chairman of the Washington-based CATO Institute said, 'The distinction between software and money is disappearing.' And nowhere is that truer than in the world of cold, hard cash."[5]

Paper money is amazing stuff. Most third world countries accept the U.S. dollar as though it was their own. If you are afraid of banks, you can still stuff it in your pillowcase and draw from it as needed. However, if you lose it, it is gone. If you don't invest, you lose potential interest and if you sit on it, you could lose its value due to inflation.

Software is transforming money. Electronic cash is sometimes called cyber cash, digital cash and smart money. Perhaps this is why Visa refers to their new microchip card as the "Smart Card." Digital money is not stored on paper, but in a group of digits that becomes programmable and smarter than paper money.

How is digital money smarter? If you send a check to your daughter at boarding school, she may spend that money for beer. But electronic cash could be debited only for certain items, such as books, car repairs or utilities. Instead of licking a stamp and going to the post office, you could send the funds electronically as an attachment to your e-mail. Time Magazine's Joshua Cooper Ramo wrote an article, "The Big Bank Theory and What it says About the Future of Money", and said, "Your daughter can store the money any way she wants, on her laptop, on a debit card, even (in the not to distant future) on a chip implanted under her skin."[6] The simple allowance has now become intelligent, budgeting only that which is helpful to the education. Plus, if lost, the digital money can be invalidated and replaced, whereas the cash would be gone.

Cyber cash has the potential to dissolve the monopoly of world governments on money. The idea is revolutionary. Wealth accounts could be programmed to loan smart money to potential borrowers all over the world who are willing to give you greater returns than a local bank. "Howard Greenspan, president of Toronto-base Heralitus Corp., a management consulting firm says: 'In the electronic city, the final step in the evolution of money is being taken. Money is being demonetized. Money is being eliminated.'"[7]

The Theory of Particle Finance

Charles Sanford Jr., the CEO of Bankers Trusts delivered a speech called, "Financial Markets in 2020." His vision is referred to as "The Theory of Particle

Finance" and has guided think tank economists since 1993, to shift the power of money to the consumer and away from institutional banks. In a sense, everyone will become a banker in the future. Your wealth account will consist of the value of any asset that has equity value (for example, the difference between what is owed on your home and what it is worth) along with savings, mutual funds, stocks and the bi-monthly income of a paycheck, minus monthly bills. The equity will allow you the opportunity to lend digital money according to your level of risk, much like your Wall Street decision to invest in a risky growth fund or a conservative bond fund.

According to Mr. Sanford, risk and reward are the two main characteristics of investments. Big risks will yield big returns, whereas safe risks yield smaller returns. For example, home mortgages are the staple of the banking industry, yielding modest annual returns of 6%. However, loans to third world countries can be very lucrative if you can stand the mental stress of defaults or government overthrows.

This world of investments via the cyber net is described like the positive and negative elements of an atom. All demands for loans would be broken up into tiny packages and marketed at various levels of risk, from small to great. Investors looking for productive returns on their digital money, could program their cyber cash to seek out interest yielding loans according to their comfort zone.

A great example is the Vanguard Total Market Index Fund. When you buy into this mutual fund, you basically own a small piece of every corporation in America. The wild swings of gain or loss by investing in any one corporation are minimized by the stability of American industry as a whole.

Charles Sanford describes the horizon as a world of financial prospects. Opportunities will abound for the average consumer, from Alaskan oil fields to distressed commercial real estate in Malaysia. "'This is like the automobile's coming,' says Sanford. 'We'd always had transportation, people walked, eventually they rode donkeys, but the automobile was a break from everything that came before it. Risk management will do that to finance. It's a total break.'"[8]

In the theory of particle finance, the household with a computer modem will become the next bank. Your mortgage, mutual fund, and savings account will become part of a huge digital universe. Your wealth account will be programmed to consider your children's college tuition the day they are born, and then invest accordingly, accounting for seasons of economic boom, bust and teenage braces. And each time you buy groceries or go to the movies, your microchip identity will draw from the wealth account, balancing the fund and directing the smart money to work on your behalf.

In Microchip We Trust

Just as confidence was essential to change from gold coins to paper certificates and then to abandon the gold standard, confidence will be essential to go from credit cards to cyber cash. The need for assurance is articulated by Fed Chairman Alan Greenspan: "The burden rests with the private industry: Regulate yourselves. 'To continue to be effective, government's regulatory role must increasingly assure that effective risk management systems are in place in the private sector.' As financial systems become more complex, detailed rules and standards have become both burdensome and ineffective." [9]

> *The theory of particle finance depends on the confidence of individuals to participate. Faith and trust are paramount.*

In other words, the theory of particle finance depends on the confidence of individuals to participate. Remember, throughout history the foundational element to the success of money, in this case the microchip identity, is the willingness of people to agree upon it as a medium of exchange. Faith and trust are paramount.

It's Just Fantasy, Right?

In the futuristic movie, *"Demolition Man"*, actors Sylvester Stallone, Wesley Snipes and Sandra Bullock are connected to society in 2030A.D. with a microchip implant in their right hand. Where does Hollywood get this stuff?

According to the London Times, as early as 1998, "Film stars and the children of millionaires were among 45 people, including several Britons, who have been approached and fitted with the chips (called the Sky Eye) in secret tests."[10] Donald G. Small, vice-president of Hughes Identification Devices of southern California stated, "Are humans running around somewhere on the globe with tags-radio-frequency tags-implanted in them? Yes! Absolutely, conclusively so!"[11]

Summary

The city where I live is growing so fast that city planners are building a second beltline around our sprawling community. The first leg of the fifty-mile beltline opened to traffic near my home. Each time I drive on the new highway, I am reminded of the microchip economy by the signs posted on each side of the road, saying "Future I-540." I find myself laughing as I cruise the new super highway, because the future is here. The signs mean the beltline will be completed in 2010, when the asphalt finally circles the metropolitan area. Likewise, the coming microchip economy is already in use. Admittedly, it has not come to full maturity, but the infrastructure is functioning in its embryonic state.

The microchip uses mentioned above are slowly eroding consumer resistance. All that remains for the microchip economy is a thin layer of skin. Just as the lion lost his majesty for the convenience of the meal, men are losing their spiritual conscience towards God for the love of money. Wherever I share this message, I find people declaring they will never accept a microchip identity implant. However, I discern multitudes will rush to embrace the identity chip in spite of their present objections. In the next chapter, we will see how marketers will persuade men to embrace the new frontier.

Four

The Snare of Benefits

"Surely, in vain the net is spread in the sight of any bird.... So are the ways of everyone who is greedy for gain; it takes away the life of the owners."
Proverbs 1:17, 19

I interviewed a patent holder for human microchip implants from the Illinois Institute of Technology who wished to remain anonymous. Interestingly, he had never heard of the mark of the beast or its biblical reference. According to him, microchip implants are great advancements for mankind. He acknowledged the technology could be used for electronic commerce via hand scanning with voluntary co-operation from the public, but dismissed any thought of nefarious motivations on the industry's part. To him, microchip implants are very beneficial.

Joseph Woodland, the inventor of the bar code for IBM, who first informed me of the universal personal identification code, also foresaw a great benefit for mankind. In fact, it is my assessment that business leaders are not caught up in any conspiracy to bring mankind into spiritual bondage or a political web of world dominance.

They are simply humble servants of the community, seeking to make life easier while making a profit.

The spirit of covetousness is the reason the microchip identity is being made possible. Covetousness is as much an expression of carnality as the spirit of violence or murder. Covetousness as a moral transgression is not as obvious as murder, but just as deadly when it causes one to receive a microchip implant to the objections of God. The snare of the microchip implant is hidden from its victims by its enormous benefit and only the discerning can grasp its unseen danger.

Identity Fraud

A great need in society is the protection of individuals from identity fraud. With today's technology, it is easy to rob someone's identity and abuse their name, credit, or wealth with nothing more than a driver's license or social security number. Information that accesses one's bank account and life can be bought on the Internet cheaply or obtained free by sorting garbage at the local dumpster.

One identity crime received national media attention. It involved a busboy armed with a cell phone, sitting at a library computer. The cyber thief used Forbes 400 list to steal personal data and defraud 217 of America's wealthiest people. His victims included Warren Buffet, Ross Perot, and Oprah Winfrey. "But it's not just the rich getting robbed, a staggering 500,000 to 700,000 Americans became the victims of identity theft last year, according to the Federal Trade Commission. This crime is growing so fast that law enforcement can't keep up."[1]

"The biggest problem in enforcement, says Jerry Coleman, an assistant district attorney in the city and county of San Francisco, is getting enough investigators to work the exploding number of fraud-related cases. 'In Los Angeles,' he says, 'the average investigator has more than 400 of these cases.'"[2]

Another scam is called "skimming." Skimming takes place when someone slides your magnetic strip card through an unauthorized handheld reader. A restaurant waiter may swipe a card's magnetic strip on his way to the cash register.

> *The average investigator in Los Angeles has more than 400 identity fraud cases.*

Overnight the account information is sold via the Internet to cyber thieves in Hong Gong, who exhaust the credit.

A young woman in our church told the story of a man who stole her identity. The thief abruptly cut his car in front of hers and slammed on the brakes. The bumpers kissed and soon he was asking for her driver's license number for insurance purposes. He promptly used her license number to open his own checking account and began writing worthless checks that were clearing the electronic credit checks because of her good name. Unfortunately in today's society, one's identity is really nothing more than a number.

Thieves are becoming more sophisticated, and technology is attempting to stay one step ahead in protecting the consumer. But as innovation comes, so comes the pressure to join the microchip revolution or be inconvenienced by the clever crook. If you lag behind in getting your microchip identity, when the thief does steal your identity and exhausts your life savings, there will be few sympathetic ears for your tale of woe. The authorities will look upon your conscientious objections as negligence.

It is estimated that one in five individuals will be victimized by identity theft in the next few years.

> *After spending hundreds of hours to restore one's name from identity theft, people will be rushing to embrace the microchip identity*

The average cost to clear one name and restore credit is $808.00 per incident. The average amount of time spent is 175 hours.[3] That is more than four weeks out of one's life.

Once you have endured the pain of losing money, the sheer hassle of getting documentation, waiting countless hours on the phone for a live person so you can tell your story, and begging for their mercy, will drive you to reconsider your spiritual convictions regarding the microchip identity. After repeated inconveniences and hundreds of hours restoring one's good name, the consumer will be rushing to embrace the microchip identity, unless of course he has the faith and patience to cleave to his convictions.[4]

It's Not Mandatory, Just Convenient

A man and his wife were planning on having their baby at home, so their child could avoid getting a social security number (SSN). The pregnancy had complications and the couple went to the hospital for assistance. The medical staff insisted the couple fill out the appropriate forms to obtain a SSN. When the couple refused, the staff said they could not leave the hospital with their baby. Is this ridiculous or what?

The husband then challenged the staff to call the social security administration and see if the law required their child had to have a SSN. It turn out that it was not absolute and off they went with their newborn child. However, the law did require the hospital *to insist* that you fill out the SSN application. This bureaucratic hassle is just the beginning of the newborn's life. The SSN is not mandatory, but incredibly controlling.

Years ago, social security cards were first printed "not for identification purposes." But try getting a job, opening a bank account or getting your electricity hooked up without one. Each time my number is requested I reply, "The government says this is not for identification, why are you asking for personal information, are you involve in identity fraud?" This really shocks people. Usually, the trouble to identify me using other means is not worth the hassle. The inconvenience slowly erodes my resolve to privacy, which is precisely the point.

The scope of government entanglements on a society can be seen in Australia's national identification card. Graham Greenleaf noted, "Every person in Australia will be required to obtain a Card, including children. The Bill does not make it legally compulsory: it simply makes it impossible for anyone to exist in Australian society without it because they will be unable to carry out normal activities…such as operation of bank accounts."[5]

The new microchip identity will insure the consumer can participate in the microchip economy without fear of identity fraud and will open the door to many new services. The marketing of these services will be a powerful inducement to receive the implanted microchip identity.

Future Benefits

The benefits of microchips are reaching as far as the imagination can dream. The following are some ideas being put forth by technology pioneers.

According to Brian Halla, CEO of National Semiconductor, in the near future businessmen will exchange business cards electronically, by merely shaking hands. The prototype is called the "Digital Handshake."[6] IBM researchers are working on this handshake concept known as PAN. It stands for "personal area network technology" to transfer data stored in a human implant. In this manner, data could be exchanged between people, or verified by an external mechanical system as a method of securing identification."[7]

Engineers with the Massachusetts Institute of Technology (MIT) have been working on "Oxygen". This five year, forty million dollar project aims to find ways to use networked devices to make computing as natural and necessary as breathing.[8] In the future, your identity chip will act as a key to open doors to your home, office or car and start an engine. Once in your apartment, the TV automatically turns on your favorite show, sensing your presence. The TV will soften its sound when the phone rings. The microwave will heat dinner precisely, communicating with the dinner's prepackaged microchip instructions and the dishwasher will automatically place an order to the manufacturer for a replacement part and schedule a repairman to visit. The refrigerator will keep track of food inventory and update the grocery list. At a voice command such as, "A night for love", the shades will turn down, soft music will begin to play and the air will be scented. And as you leave, the thermostat will adjust the room's temperature to save money in your absence.

> *Professor Kevin Warwick of England successfully tested the "Connected Society" by implanting himself with a microchip to communicate with his household appliances*

This vision is sometimes referred to as the "Connected Society" and was tested by Professor Kevin Warwick of

England by implanting himself with a microchip to successfully communicate with his household appliances.[9]

Medical Benefits

The implanted microchip is finding many uses in the medical field. As early as 1993, the "Safe Medical Devices Registration Act required all medical implants in humans to be identified with a rice size biochip, the same kind that is being implanted in animals. In the October, 1994 issue of Popular Science, an article titled "Future Watch: Body Binary" predicted, "Within ten years, we'll have miniature computers inside us to monitor and perhaps control our blood pressure, heart rate and cholesterol."[10]

My niece who recently graduated from LaGrange as a registered nurse, confirmed that professors are discussing implanted microchips for the purpose of keeping a patient's medical records. The microchip has a read-write capability that would "carry a person's medical history, and as that history evolved the subsequent information could also be added to the microchip."[11]

Global Tracking

The microchip can be used in conjunction with the Global Positioning Satellite system (GPS). This technology is used in the "On Star" systems of new vehicles. You press a button and a voice inquires from a monitoring station concerning your need. This technology can be used for luggage tags and according to one IBM executive, is installed in all new laptop computers. Its tracking function is used by car rental agencies to track their cars and fine speeding motorists, and trucking companies locate their trucks and delivery packages, and determine how long employees stop for lunch.[12] Denver attached tracking chips to their snowplows and discovered productivity increased fifty percent.

According to the Arizona Republic, Jack Dunlap, a private investigator in Tucson, Arizona, tried to launch a program called KIDSCAN. Kids would get a biochip implant for the purpose of GPS monitoring. Parents could locate their kids at the mall by looking at a GPS monitor. With the GPS function parents would know via the Internet where their teenagers were with the family car. Did they go to the friend's house to spend the night like they said, or did they go to the beach for the weekend?

The GPS feature would allow governments to monitor criminals with house arrest. In 1999, Governor Gary Johnson of New Mexico "raised the possibility that a futuristic form of incarceration could include implanting microchips in convicted felons. This would help solve the problem of New Mexico's overcrowded prisons."[13]

The microchip identity will function just like a CD which has computer read and read-write capability. The future chip will be downloaded with enormous amounts of information. By receiving the microchip identity, you will no longer have to remember passwords, pin numbers, employment history, what medicines you are allergic too, past medical treatments or anything else downloaded onto your hand's identity chip.

The microchip's information could alert employers to criminal backgrounds of job applicants for sensitive positions such as pilots, security guards and day care workers. "If a police officer made a routine traffic stop, the individual could be quickly scanned to see if he had a nefarious background."[14]

"If I Only Had a Brain"

The benefits are incredible. Its no wonder Visa advertised their "Smart Card" with a melody from the "Wizard of Oz." When the scarecrow reached the wizard, he requested, "If I only had a brain." The ad's visual image was a microchip coming from the heavens, inserting itself into a "Smart Card" for the happy consumer, as the catchy tune climaxed with, "If I only had a brain."

> *In the future ads will say, "Why Carry Plastic?" Suggesting microchip implantation*

Summary

In the years to come, savvy marketers are going to expound the benefits of the microchip identity. The subtle communication will advocate the smart thing to do is to "Get Chipped." Its convenience will be a seductive snare to the unwary and in the future the ads will say, "Why Carry Plastic?" suggesting microchip implantation.

Five

The Declaration of Detriments

"The door of wisdom swings on hinges of common sense and uncommon thoughts." William Arthur Ward

When the colonists penned the Declaration of Independence from the King of England, they wrote, "A decent respect to the opinions of mankind requires that they should declare the causes which impel them to the separation." Likewise, refusing to join the masses in receiving the microchip identity, I must explain my reservations.

The evolution of money reveals the development of man's faith in various forms of money. It has only been just over a hundred years since man transitioned from coins, to accept paper money backed by silver and gold. It has only been fifty years since man began to use plastic credit cards and twenty-five years since the government lifted the gold standard. And it has only been a couple of years since plastic cards with microchips have been introduced. This is a short time period compared to the history of trust man has placed in silver and gold.

Two thousand years ago a prophet name John said that men would buy and sell with a mark in their right hand just before the revealing of Jesus Christ.[1] For two thousand years this idea has seemed absurd. Yet this incredible prophecy is coming true in our lifetime. In the millenniums of time, it has only been in the past few years, that men have departed from silver and gold. Ironically or should I say prophetically, the new money is in perfect alignment with the prophet's warning. The evolution of microchip money is evidence we are in the last days prior to the appearing of Jesus Christ.

Another prophet Daniel wrote concerning the last days, "Seal up the book until the time of the end; many shall run to and fro, and knowledge shall increase."[2] The microchip is a magnificent display of the ingenuity of man. Its circuits are loaded with knowledge. And wherever men run worldwide, their smart money is accepted.

God has my attention! His spiritual roadmap is clear. His warning is the judgment of hell for those who accept the microchip into their right hand or forehead.[3] For this reason, I am a *spiritual conscientious objector*." This is the greatest detriment of the microchip identity: it has eternal consequences that violate the spiritual conscience of Bible adherents.

Government Ownership

The colonists further wrote in the Declaration of Independence, "Governments are instituted among Men, deriving their just powers from the Consent of the Governed...." Eventually, the microchip identity will become mandatory.[4] To embrace the system is to lay the foundation of despotism from which our forefathers fought to free themselves from.

To accept the microchip as mandatory is to go from "government by the people" to "government ownership of the people." Hence, instead of people giving privileges to the government, the government grants rights to the people. The people are then treated as a national resource.

> *To accept the microchip identity is to lay the foundation of despotism from which our forefathers fought to free themselves from.*

Just after the terrorist attack on the World Trade Towers in New York City, the question raised most often was, "What freedoms do Americans need to relinquish, to resume normal life as quickly as possible." Stephen Flynn, a spokesman for the Council on Foreign Relations, was interviewed by Peter Jennings of ABC News. When asked what security measures airports needed to thwart terrorism, Mr. Flynn responded, "Install iris-scan machines."

These machines are part of the infrastructure of the microchip identity to confirm an individual's identity. It does so by confirming the bio-metric value of the iris to the numeric value engraved on the implanted microchip, thus yielding a positive identification. Otherwise, a terrorist could simply kill an individual, surgically remove the microchip and insert the chip in his own hand.

The change is subtle, but oppressive. Innocent travelers will go to the airport to prove they are not terrorists, by subjecting themselves to an identity scan. Authorities will tap into a database to measure one's history of good versus evil. Fundamentally, courts have treated citizens as innocent until proven guilty, but now citizens will be treated as guilty until proven innocent. The difference is the burden of proof and strips the conscience of freedom.

During each scan, one's conscience will ponder its past and present behavior. Authorities will know of your night in jail for public drunkenness or misdemeanor for an adolescent crime. Worry of past indiscretions will drain the emotions and bring a whole new dimension to public anxiety.

But if you want to be expedited through the airport, you will need to get chipped to avoid inconveniences. This new process is being referred to as the safe or trusted traveler program and is modeled after successful airports in the middle-east.

Offices to Harass

The colonists wrote this grievance to King George in The Declaration of Independence, "He has erected a multitude of New Offices, and sent hither swarms of Officers to harass our people...." Having a microchip implant at the disposal of employers, insurance agencies, schools, hospitals and police will result in a great loss of privacy and make vital information vulnerable through government data banks.

The insurance company will know if heart attacks run in the family's history or if one's DNA holds a propensity toward diabetes. The potential employer will know if you have been guilty of shoplifting, and the university will know if you have been expelled from high school when reviewing your application.

People change, grow, and mature spiritually and emotionally. Their character should not be blighted by unforgiving pasts or misunderstandings. It is not the nature of God to mark iniquities.[5] But it is the nature of Satan to accuse.[6] This subtle atmosphere of pointing the finger is the same harassing spirit our founding fathers were trying to prevent. Their constitution provided for privacy in the fourth amendment: "The right of the people to be secure in their persons, houses, papers, and effects, against unreasonable searches and seizures, shall not be violated..." A peaceful conscience is foundational to freedom.

Most Americans would be alarmed at the prospect of a national ID if they understood the ramifications. In "police states" the ID is not really about identity, but authorization.

> *In "police states" the ID is not really about identity, but authorization.*

In essence, one has to have the favor of the state to work, travel, buy a house, or get medical care.

Authorization could be denied for reasons such as being a deadbeat parent, delinquent in taxes, failure to pay parking tickets, database errors and any other social controls that the government decided to attach to the system. When an individual uses the ID for any transaction, he is basically asking "Big Brother" for permission.

Outside Control

I once made a substantial down payment on a piece of land with a home equity check. The next day I used the home equity card to make a small purchase in Wal-Mart. The cashier informed me that my account had been frozen. Bewildered and embarrassed, I put the item back because I had no cash. The credit company had shut down my account because of the previous transaction.

The microchip identity will have the same capabilities. An outside authority will have the ability to inactivate the chip. This simple act will have enormous ramifications in the absence of alternative ways to pay.

When the eventual microchip economy is under world domination by the Anti-Christ, the individual will be very conscientious of his thoughts and attitudes towards the tyrannical leader. After all, it would be a terrible thing to walk into a grocery store and discover your wealth account had been frozen because of your cynical attitude toward the governing authority. The cold war citizens of the former Soviet Union experienced this oppressive atmosphere. Their fear of government reprisals caused them to hold their tongues, thus quenching freedom of expression. The resulting public atmosphere was one of fear and intimidation.

Privacy Invaders

The GPS ability of the microchip identity is an invasion of privacy. Does an individual really want someone knowing where they are at all times? Where you went for your honeymoon or vacation. Someone could follow your movements every time you leave the home or office.

The Department of Transportation now airs all of its TV cameras on our interstate highways via the Internet. Other security departments have public cameras in heavily traveled areas such as parks, courthouses and public facilities. With GPS following your every movement, it is conceivable that someone could follow your car through the streets, to the parking deck of the local mall and as you walk from store to store via the internet. This blanket of attention is suffocating.

World Despotism

The colonist believed, "All men are created equal, that they are endowed by their Creator with certain unalienable Rights, that among these are Life, Liberty and the pursuit of Happiness." They further asserted the role of government was to enhance its citizen's pursuit of safety and happiness.

The lesson of the colonists with King George is a lesson to be remembered for the future Anti-Christ. The colonist understood a familiar truth, "Absolute power corrupts absolutely." Their Declaration of Independence stated: "The history of the present King of Great Britain is a history of repeated injuries and usurpations, all having in direct object the establishment of absolute Tyranny over these States."

> *The lesson of the colonists with King George is a lesson to be remembered for the future Anti-Christ*

They further admonished the king, "When a long train of abuses and usurpations...evinces a design to reduce them under absolute Despotism, it is their right, it is their duty, to throw off such Government, and to provide new Guards for their future security."

> *In the absence of leadership, people slowly raise a white flag to bureaucratic encroachment, while clinging to their diminished freedoms*

The question is; what *are* the best solutions for procuring "Life, Liberty and the pursuit of Happiness" and the "New Guards of future security." In the absence of leadership and solutions, people slowly raise a white flag to bureaucratic encroachment, while clinging to their diminished freedoms. Part III is God's solution.

The Microchip Solution

Social architects keep proposing their solutions to "the pursuit of life and liberty". Tim Willard, Executive Officer of the World Future Society, a Washington, DC based organization that claims 27,000 members worldwide suggests using biochip implants in humans. Mr. Willard said, "A number could be assigned at birth and go with a person throughout life...the biochip would be implanted in the back of the hand so that it would be easy to scan...at the checkout stand at the super market, you would simply pass your hand over a scanner and your bank account would automatically be debited."[7]

Scott Hodge wrote an article for the Los Angeles Daily Journal and echoed this sentiment. The headline alone was chilling, "Big Brother's I.D. Card Better Yet, Why Not Just Brand Babies?" A Northwestern University sociologist named Bernard Beck said, "If I have a universal ID [chip] implanted, I can cash a check anywhere in the world... The notion of using implantable chips to control humans isn't entirely absent, even in these early stages of the technology's development."[8]

Other newspapers have run articles predicting the microchip identity. The headline of the Wenztville Journal, Wentzville, Missouri, read, "St. Peters Mayor Gets Earful of Ire over Talk of Microchip." The article said Mayor Tom Brown wanted to inject everyone's ear with an ID microchip. Another headline for the Tucson Citizen's newspaper read, "Magazine Predicts Future of Society." The article discussed, "An ID chip will be implanted in our bodies...that will replace your driver's license, credit card and other forms of ID." One of the oldest newspapers in America is the Chicago Tribune. Their headline read, "In Future; Tiny Chip May Get

Under Skin" with a subtitle, "Critics Argue The Device Invites Big Brother."[9] The article said a microchip would be available as a consumer item in the twenty-first century. Indeed it is!

Each relinquished freedom is consumed by the intrusion of big brother. Eventually when fully implemented, big brother's microchip identity will have the same oppressive nature ascribed to King George. In the Declaration of Independence, the colonists described the king's abuse of power as, "The sole purpose of fatiguing them into compliance with his measures."

The end result of the microchip identity is not one of freedom, but of slavery. Big Brother's control will not liberate the conscience, but suppress it. Freedom of religion will not be of choice, but a disingenuous reverence for the government, lest one's wealth account be suspended. This oppression will denigrate the human spirit, as souls appease the Anti-Christ as their source of sustenance. The spirit of free men will soon be likened to the lifeless Jews of Nazi Germany under Hitler, who were tattooed with numbers on their inner arm.

Like the lion stripped of his majesty, freedom will be caged. Men will slowly give away rights grasping for life, only to find they lose life, just as Jesus said.[10] Because of the love of money, their voluntary compliance will be a slow spiritual suicide, like a chain smoker, culminating in spiritual death.[11]

Summary

The proponents of the microchip identity will trumpet its benefits and the multitudes will blindly follow. But the Psalmist said, "Every story sounds good, 'til you hear the other side."[12] Jesus said, "Wide is the gate and broad is the way that leads to destruction, and there are many who go in by it" and "Narrow is the gate and difficult is the way which leads to life, and there are few who find it."[13]

The consensus will argue, what else can we do, we must have unity, we must have security, and we must go forward with change. Anatole France once said, "If fifty million people say a foolish thing, it is still a foolish thing." An old adage appropriately fits the microchip identity; "He who does not learn from the past is doomed to repeat it."

The Declaration of Independence is a testimony to the cravings of settlers for freedom from an oppressive king. Their signatures placed fortunes, lives and family at risk of death and imprisonment from the wrath of King George. Those bold and courageous pioneers were willing to lay down their lives for freedom. Like King George, the Anti-Christ will seek to kill those who refuse his authority.[14] We must be bold and courageous.

Are you ready for the other side? Are you willing to lay down your life, so you may obtain life as Jesus said?[15] God promises, "If My People who are called by My name will humble themselves, and turn from their wicked ways, then I will hear from heaven, and will forgive their sin and heal their land."[16] It will require a pioneering spirit, for "The just shall live by faith."[17] Like the settlers of New England, we will be pilgrims seeking a new land where God promises freedom.[18]

In Part II, we will discover the ancient cult of the golden calf. If we are going to repent, we must understand the evil spirit gripping our nation. America, like Israel of old has been sidetracked on the way to the promised land by the worship of the golden calf. Once repented, revival will come and America's glory will shine again.

Part II

The Golden Calf

"They made a calf… and worshiped the molded image. Thus they changed their glory into the image of an ox that eats grass. They forgot God their Savior who had done great things…."
Psalm 106:19-21

Six

Why Worship A Cow?

*"The Cow is Heaven, the Cow is Earth,
the Cow is Vishnu, Lord of Life"*
Atharva Veda X:10

Why worship a cow? Gosh, the very thought is bewildering. Stop by any pasture to observe bovine behavior and ponder. How could any person, people or nation, think this is a god? They must see more than I am viewing. The cow stands by the fence, chewing her nasty cud as saliva drools. Snot oozes from her nostrils as four stomachs churn the grass, pausing for an occasional belch to upchuck more cud. Putrefying waste is smeared down the backside of her hind parts. The tail swishes flies, spreading the foul back and forth to her flanks, filling the air with an obnoxious scent of dung. The hide is crusty from lying in the dirt, making the fur coarse and stiff. Suddenly the tail lifts and spouts urine into the very field she is grazing. The split hoofs sink into the oozing mud as she innocently pleads compassionate strokes from her visitors proclaiming, "Behold your god...Yuk!"

But, "beauty is in the eye of the beholder." To understand the ancient worship of cows, we must look through the eyes of early nomads and see beyond our twenty first century urban culture.

Astrology's Cow Worship

> *We must look through the eyes of early nomads and see beyond our twenty first century urban culture to understand why men worshipped the cow*

The earliest mention of cattle is on the sixth day of creation.[1] The cow's uniqueness made it the only animal mentioned by name. Adam and Eve must have agreed the cow's milk, cheese and butter were a delightful diversion from the green herbs that God had given for food. After the flood of Noah, God allowed men to eat animals.[2] The smell of beef, roasting over the evening fire made the cow a complete food source.

After a delicious meal, nomads pondered the heavens and perhaps with gratitude, saw in the stars the image of a bull. The Taurus bull is one of the oldest symbols of the Zodiac constellations dating back 6000 years. Astrologers know from early literature, "the bull was one of the early animal gods of Chaldeans, Egyptians and other nearby lands. Perhaps it was for that reason that the image of the bull was so common on temple walls, boundary stones, coins and jewelry in ancient Greece and Egypt. Of all the constellations, Taurus reigned supreme in the band that contained the planetary gods circling the heavens while other luminaries maintained fixed patterns."[3]

Egyptian and Mesopotamian Cows

"In many areas of the world the cow is the primary dairy animal. Its production of milk makes it a symbol of gentle, nourishing motherhood, abundance and fertility. Because it provides milk for humans, the cow is, in a way, the nurse mother of humankind and so she is considered symbolic of "mother earth." In fact, the legs of Nut, Egypt's "Celestial Cow," are mythically the four quarters of the earth."[4] "The Egyptian nature goddess "Isis" is considered the daughter of the sky god, Nut. Isis is frequently represented with a cow's head or horns."[5]

"Even though the cow is a very earthy symbol, the crescent-shaped horns make her an ancient symbol of the moon. Many lunar and mother goddesses around the world wear cow's horns on their heads. The moon personified is sometimes pictured riding the skies in a chariot pulled by a cow."[6]

"The bull was a widespread symbol of the gods in the ancient Near East. In Egypt the bull was a symbol of the fertility god, Apis. In Mesopotamia the storm god, Ishkur/Adad is called "bull of heaven" and "grand bull." In mythological texts from the ancient city of Ugarit, the bull is associated with the high god, El, symbolizing both strength and fertility."[7]

Hindu Cow Worship

Many scholars believe the Rig Veda scriptures of the Hindu are the oldest writings of man. "From very early times, the cow was revered as the possessor of great power. This is the natural reaction of an agricultural people to an animal valuable for plowing, transportation, fertilizer, and food...the cow and her manifold useful properties provided a peculiarly satisfying object for identification. In early Hindu cultures, Indians sacrificed the cows and ate the meat, whereas now, few will consider even tasting the flesh."[8] "The cow became important in India, first in the Vedic Period (1500-900 BC), but only as a symbol of wealth. For the Vedic man, cows were the 'real life' substratum of the goods of life."[9]

> *The cow became important in India, first in the Vedic Period (1500-1900 BC), but only as a symbol of wealth*

"Even today, among devout Hindus, the cow is considered a sacred animal and may not be injured. In Vedic tradition, when people die, their souls are led along the Milky Way to the Kingdom of the Blessed by celestial cows. One of the chores of the dead is to frequently sacrifice [to] the divine "Cow of Abundance."

This heavenly cow is actually a cloud which when sacrificed provides rain for the earth's crops. The cow also provides the dust or "milk" of the Milky Way, which is believed to nourish the earth. The "Cow of Abundance" is also known as the "Melodious Cow" because of a tradition similar to the Judeo-Christian belief that the earth was created from a divine sound or Word."[10]

The following verses in praise of the cow are taken from a Hindu hymn, where through a process of mystical identifications, the cow becomes the whole visible universe:[11]

> Worship to thee, springing to life, and worship to thee when born! Worship, O Cow, to thy tail-hair, and to thy hooves, and to thy form!
> Hitherward we invite with prayer the Cow who pours a thousand streams, By whom the heaven,

by whom the earth, by whom these waters are preserved... Forth from thy mouth the songs came, from thy neck's nape sprang strength, O Cow.

Sacrifice from thy flanks was born, and rays of sunlight from thy teats. From thy fore-quarters and thy thighs motion was generated, Cow! Food from thine entrails was produced, and from thy belly came the plants.... They call the Cow immortal life, pay homage to the Cow as Death.

She hath become this universe, Fathers, and Rishis, hath become the Gods, and men, and Spirits. The man who hath this knowledge may receive the Cow with welcoming. So for the giver willingly doth perfect sacrifice pour milk....

The Cow is Heaven, the Cow is Earth, the Cow is Vishnu, Lord of Life. The heavenly beings have drunk the out-pourings of the Cow. When these heavenly beings have drunk the out-pourings of the Cow, they in the Bright One's dwelling-place pay adoration to her milk. For Soma, some have milked her: some worship the fatness she hath poured. They who have given a cow to him who hath this knowledge have gone up to the third region of the sky. He who hath given a Cow unto the Brahmans winneth all the worlds. For Right is firmly set in her, devotion, and religious zeal.

Both Gods and mortal men depend for life and being on the Cow. She hath become this universe: all that the Sun surveys is she.

Atharva Veda X:10

It is easy to see from this ancient writing that Hindu nomads rejoiced in the cow, a creature enormously versatile in providing food. In my research, I spoke with a

Hindu elder and he confirmed the cow's worship. He shared with me that even today many Hindu see the cow's urine as medicinal. They use the urine to splash on their bodies, comb into their hair, and drink for its health benefits. Does this sound unbelievable? *Ripley's Believe it or Not* has a video piece showing the practice. One visitor to my home confirmed his grandparents drink cow urine everyday.

> *"Who exchanged the truth of God for the lie, and worshiped and served the creature rather than the Creator."*
> *-Apostle Paul*

Unfortunately, early cultures made a spiritual mistake that haunts generations. The Apostle Paul acknowledged this misdirected reverence when he wrote of those, "Who exchange the truth of God for the lie, and worshiped and served the creature rather than the Creator."[12]

In this present generation, many will make the same mistake when they accept the microchip identity. Their thought will lament, "How will I be able to buy or sell, how will I survive?" They will accept "the lie." Their acceptance of the identity chip will be an act of worship born of ignorance, as they acknowledge the chip as their source of sustenance.

The Prophetic Hindu Mark?

An ancient Hindu practice, dating before Moses, is eerie if not prophetic. Forbes in his *Oriental Memoirs* says, "In India different idolatrous sects have different marks [for their bodies]. These are especially common among the two principal sects, the worshippers of Siva and the worshippers of Vishnoo. The marks are horizontal and perpendicular lines; crescents [symbol of cow horns] or circles; or representations of leaves, eyes, and other objects. They are impressed on the forehead by the officiating Brahmin with a composition of sandal-wood dust and oil, or the ashes of *cow-dung* and turmeric. The colors are red, black, white, and yellow. In many cases these marks are renewed daily."[13]

The Brahmin's adhesive cow-manure expresses their reverence for the cow as "lord of life." When the mark on the forehead is a crescent shape symbol for horns, the cow's worship is further accentuated. This certainly adds new meaning to the phrase, "mark of the beast."

The Brahmin presses the mark on the Hindu forehead with a composition of cow-dung ashes. Is this ancient practice prophetic of the "mark of the beast?"

Perhaps this ancient practice is what Moses was referring too when he wrote, "They have corrupted themselves, their spot is not the spot of his [God's] children: they are a perverse and crooked generation. Do ye thus requite the Lord, O foolish people and unwise? Is not he [God] thy father that hath bought thee? Hath he not made thee, and established thee?"[14]

The Apostle John spoke of the Anti-Christ's mark on the forehead or hand as a demonic deception. John said, "He deceived those who received the mark of the beast and those who worshiped his image."[15]

The book of Job is the oldest known Scripture of Jews and Christians. The book dates back to just after the flood of Noah. Perhaps Job was referring to this ancient middle-eastern ritual when he justified himself to his accusers by denying, "a spot was on his hand."[16]

Either way, the spot on the forehead of the Hindu is a constant reminder the Anti-Christ will eventually try to implement a worldwide mark. That mark is a spiritual deception, designed to draw men's allegiance to the Anti-Christ as their source and not God, just as the Brahmin reminds the Hindu of the cow's sustenance.

The Cow as Wealth and Prosperity

Before the time of coinage, Abraham and Job's wealth was described by being very rich in cattle.[17] When Laban paid Jacob wages, it was in the form of livestock. And cattle as wealth can be seen in Israel's victory over the Midianites in the desert after the Exodus. The cattle were described as spoil and booty, the valuables taken from the defeated enemy.[18]

When God spoke of Israel's journey to the promised land, he described it as a "land flowing with milk and honey." The milk is understood to be the product of an abundance of grass for the cows to graze.[19] When the prodigal son returned home to his father, the family celebrated by feasting on the fatted calf.[20] Stalled calves were fattened for special occasions and were considered a luxury.[21] When God brought the ten plagues upon Egypt, he made a distinction in the cattle. The severe pestilence caused the Egyptian cows to die, but the Hebrew cows were immune.[22] This plague was a severe judgment on the prosperity of the Egyptian. Yet God preserved the Hebrew's wealth.

God demanded in the law, that merchants use just weights in their commerce.[23] The influence of cattle on wealth can be seen near the city of Thebes in Egypt. In a tomb nearby is a (circa) 15th century BC painting depicting an Egyptian weighing gold rings on a balance. The rings are measured against weights that are molten in the shape of a bull's head to determine their value.[24]

Finally, Joseph interpreted Pharaoh's dream of seven fat cows being devoured by seven thin cows, followed by seven full heads of stalk being consumed by seven blighted heads of stalk. Joseph understood the culture's reverence for the wealth of cattle. Therefore it is logical that Joseph easily received from God the interpretation; seven years of bumper crops were coming for the economy, followed by seven years of famine.[25]

The Cow's Enduring Influence

God gave the cow as a gift to mankind, a wonderful source of food. Ancient cultures reveal how man's thankfulness gradually slipped into the worship of the creature, more than the Creator. To this day conversational phrases such as, *"Holy Cow"* or *"Sacred Cow"* find their roots in ancient religious practices.

> *Conversational phrases such as "Holy Cow" and "Sacred Cow" find their roots in ancient religious practices*

The importance of the cow as a source of food can be seen in the pilgrims of New England and Jamestown. Cows are not indigenous to America, but were brought here by Christopher Columbus. The Spanish government required one cow for every five settlers to be brought on Columbus' second journey.[26]

The influence of the cow as wealth is very much a part of our present English language. As mentioned before, the word *pecuniary*, meaning monetary comes from the Latin word *pecus*, meaning cow. A cattle rancher called to my attention several terms that demonstrate the cow's influence on economics. The word *capital*, meaning the value of assets, comes from the word cattle. A *chattel mortgage* is a bank note that is guaranteed by one's livestock and of course we have all heard the phrase "*Cash Cow*", meaning a quick way to get money.[27] The word "*stock*" in the banner, "Wall Street Stock Market" is a lingering reference to the value of cattle or livestock.

Bulls: Symbols of Power

In the ancient land of Canaan, there were many gods referred to as "Baal". "The word Baal signifies lord, not in the sense of a ruler, but as the possessor or owner of a region." The common symbol of the Baal was a bull.[28] The bull symbolized the "strength, vigor and endurance"[29] of the spirit that governed the region. Thus, people with certain affections for a carnal appetite were drawn to regions with the same spirit.

For example, the governing spirit over Nashville is easily recognized as a spirit of music. The spirit of New Orleans is one of party and revelry. The spirit of Amsterdam is sensuality. The same is true for countries. The spirit of Columbia is drugs. In France the spirit is romance. Organizations can reflect a spirit as well. The Islamic Taliban was infamous for its spirit of violence and terrorism, whereas the American Red Cross is known for its spirit of compassion and benevolence.

One of the best known symbols in America is the Wall Street Bull

Perhaps one of the best-known symbols in America is the Wall Street Bull. This Baal-bull symbolizes the spirit of American capitalism and the investor's desire to have an expanding "bullish" economy. Foreigners immigrate to America with the dream of starting a business to get rich and enjoy prosperity.

The "Bulls of Bashan"

When King Og of Bashan came against the Hebrews in battle, God delivered the king along with the land.[30] Og was a mighty king and the victory was great for several reasons. Bashan was called the "land of the giants". King Og was huge, his bed was thirteen feet long and six feet wide.[31] Also, Bashan was known for its green pastures and the tribes of Rueben and Gad received the land as an inheritance from God because they had much livestock.[32] The victory became a symbol of Israel's strength and they sang of the triumph in their worship.[33] The lyrical phrase, "Bulls of Bashan" reflected the strength and power of that victory and the wealth of pastureland for cattle.

David, when fleeing from the oppression of King Saul, lamented, "Many bulls have suppressed Me; Strong bulls of Bashan have encircled Me."[34] David in his distress used this descriptive phrase to acknowledge the power and strength of the corrupt king's might. David by his humble submission, patiently waited on the Lord, and God removed King Saul and his oppressive government.

The prophet Amos used the phrase, "cows of Bashan"[35] to describe the women of Samaria during Israel's backslidden condition. They had become greedy, lazy and given to drinking. They added to their guilt by oppressing the poor and needy. The prophet's phrase "cows of Bashan" was meant to express the strength of the spirit they were following (cows are the feminine versus bulls for male). Unfortunately, Israel did not repent and God took them captive to Babylon for seventy years, to teach them not to follow the spirit of covetousness.

Summary

Down through history, mankind has worshipped the cow for several reasons. First, he was grateful for the milk, cheese, meat and leather for food and clothing. Secondly, the herds represented wealth and third, that wealth gave power. Perhaps ignorantly, but nonetheless, man succumbed to worshipping the creature more than the Creator as his source of sustenance.

When the Anti-Christ reveals himself, the Bible says he "Exalts himself above all that is called God or that is worshiped, so that he sits as God, in the temple of God, showing himself that he is God."[36] When he implements the microchip identity by making it mandatory, the receiving of the chip is an act of worship. The chip sits in the temple of God (your body).[37] The chip in essence proclaims, the Anti-Christ is my source of sustenance, his identity chip accesses my wealth account to buy and sell, and it allows me to increase in financial strength, giving me greater power and dominion.

The spirit of the microchip identity and the cow are the same. Carnal men will worship his creation more than the Creator. The worship is directly attached to the microchip's ability to give sustenance, just as the cow provided nourishment to early nomad.

Seven

The Golden Calf

"He received the gold... fashioned it with an engraving tool, and made a molded calf. Then they said, 'This is your god, O Israel, that brought you out of the land of Egypt!'" Exodus 32:4

When the Hebrew prepared to enter the promised land, God gave them this explanation for choosing them. "The Lord your God has chosen you to be a people for Himself, a special treasure above all the people of the earth. The Lord did not set His love on you nor choose you because you were more in number than any other people, for you were the least of all peoples; but because the Lord loves you, and because He would keep the oath which He swore to your fathers..."[1] Unfortunately the Hebrew became disillusioned and decided to make themselves a god. The image they chose was a golden calf. Their destiny was to conquer the promised land to the glory of God. Instead, they succumbed to the carnality of calf worship like the pagan nations.

Moses tells the story of the golden calf and Stephen retells the story in the New Testament (Exodus 32 and Acts 7:37-43). Here is a brief summary. Moses ascended the mountain to receive God's laws. While "Moses delayed in coming", Aaron the priest was pressured to make the people a god. He took from each of them earrings of gold and fashioned a molten image of a calf. They proclaimed the "golden calf to be the god" who delivered them from Egypt. Aaron announced a "feast unto the Lord" and the people "rose up to play" and party over the work of their hands. The disloyalty prompted God to anger. Through intercession for the people, Moses influenced Him to relent of immediate wrath, but God promised to "blot out" the transgressors from His book of life.

Referring to this event, the Apostle Paul said, "Now all these things happened to them as examples, and they were written for our admonition, upon whom the ends of the ages have come."[2] The story of the golden calf reveals four important characteristics about the last days. Although men will not worship an actual golden calf, the spirit of reverence for the microchip identity is the same.

Parallel One: Christ Delays in Coming

Moses spoke of a time when "God will raise up for you a Prophet like me from your brethren. Him you shall hear."[3] Stephen said this prophet was Jesus, who is like Moses in several ways. Like Moses, Jesus performed signs and wonders. He is the mediator between God and man, and Jesus (like Moses) has delayed in coming.

The Apostle Peter said, "Scoffers will come in the last days, walking according to their own lusts, and saying, 'Where is the promise of His coming?'"[4] These last days are revealing a growing sense of hopelessness. Many have predicted the return of Christ and each date seems to come and go. Each build up of anticipation is dashed and the people sigh, "all things continue as they were from the beginning." This spirit of despair is causing people to walk in unbelief and turn to their own devices.

The people should be patiently waiting, anticipating God's commands and preparing themselves to obey His will. Instead, people are finding solace in alternative religions, lifestyles and jobs. The heart of man is created to worship and he is seeking for a god to pour himself into. Man is looking for a god who will give the world a sense of identification, security and sustenance in their wilderness experience.

Parallel Two: The Golden Calf is God

A carpenter and a goldsmith made the golden calf. First, the carpenter shaped the wood into the image of a calf. Secondly, the goldsmith hammered out flat sheets of gold and then used engraving tools to fashion the gold to the wooden idol. The finished product was a piece of wood with an outward appearance of precious gold.[5]

The Hebrew succumbed to the spirit of the false religions around them. The descendents of Abraham were shepherds and their "occupation had been to feed livestock from their youth."[6] They too believed *"the lie"* that somehow the milk, cheese, meat and leather products were their source of sustenance and not God. Suddenly they were trusting the wealth of their herds and "Exchanged the truth of God for the lie, and worshiped and served the creature rather than the Creator..."[7]

The spirit is the same in these last days. As a pastor, I am weary of people who excuse themselves from worship because they are tired and need rest from their week of work. Their behavior exposes their heart, work and the subsequent cars, homes and pleasures the income purchases is first in their life; God is secondary. If they gave their employer the same attendance they give to God, they would be fired.

> *"It is the Lord who gives you the power to make wealth"*

Moses forewarned of this very attitude, "Beware that you do not forget the Lord your God...lest when you have eaten and are full, and have built beautiful houses and dwell in them...and your silver and your gold are multiplied...then you say in your heart, 'My power and the might of my hand have gained me this wealth.'...remember the Lord your God, for it is He who gives you power to get wealth, that He may establish His covenant...."[8]

The Hebrew appeared pious. They had a priest who pacified their false piety by not insisting on the diligent attendance of God's commands. The idol was impressive; the exterior of finely engraved gold, glistening in the noonday sun was glorious and made them feel good about themselves. When men package themselves in beautiful new cars, name brand clothing and magnificent custom homes, they feel superior. They say to themselves, I am a good person, look at all I have.

However, as a pastor, I am appalled that professing believers routinely skip the weekly worship of God, only to find out later they adored their car with wax, uplifted their real estate by manicuring the lawn, or glorified their body with sun-worship at the beach. These shallow believers have become like the golden calf they worship.

The Bible says, "The Lord does not see as man sees; for man looks at the outward appearance, but the Lord looks at the heart."[9] The golden calf idol was impressive on the outside, but it was made of wood on the inside. Jesus forewarned of this pious outward appearance with righteous indignation, "For you cleanse the outside of the cup and dish, but inside are full of …self indulgence. Blind Pharisee, first cleanse the inside of the cup and dish, that the outside …may be clean also…you outwardly appear righteous to men, but inside you are full of …lawlessness."[10] These are harsh words. Should men be concerned?

The Apostle Paul forewarns, "In the last days perilous times will come: For men will be lovers of themselves, lovers of money… lovers of pleasure rather than lovers of God, having a form of godliness but denying its power."[11]

> *To habitually put money and pleasure before God will develop a yielding spirit to the microchip identity so you can continue a materialistic lifestyle*

Why is this kind of attitude perilous? To habitually put money and pleasure before God will develop a yielding spirit to the microchip identity so you can continue a materialistic lifestyle. Jesus said, "For what profit is it to a man if he gains the whole world, and loses his own soul? Or what shall a man give in exchange for his soul? For whoever desires to save his life will lose it, but whoever loses his life for My sake will find it."[12]

Parallel Three: Rose up to Play

The Hebrew had spent four hundred years in Egypt. While there, they observed the idolatrous worship of the "Egyptian bulls of Apis in Memphis and Mnevis in On. The worship was accompanied with lascivious dances and other obscene practices."[13] The backslidden Hebrew followed the Egyptian pattern in their worship of the golden calf. Absurdly, they called it a "feast unto the Lord."

> *"What a confused, upside down view of success. Yet multitudes still strive for it."*
> *-David Wilkerson*

The spirit is the same today. Much discussion has been spent on a teenage pop star, which accompanies her concerts with sensual dance and provocative dress. The media applauds her for being a "role model" to young Christian girls and defends her lascivious conduct as freedom of expression. Its seems that as long as the conduct brings you wealth, fame and pleasure, its okay. "It does not matter if the behavior leads multitudes down the same path of moral destruction and ruins innocent people who follow. She will still be judged a success by the world's standards. What a confused, upside-down view of success. Yet multitudes still strive for it."[14]

As a pastor, I follow the admonitions of the Apostle Paul, "to do the work of an evangelist." One evangelistic outreach consists of going to the local university's football games, to share with tailgaters about the love of Jesus. I put on my shirt with the phrase "Jesus Saves" emblazoned on the back in bold letters. As I approach the small groups of ten and twenty students gathered around their social peers, I ask a simple question, "Have you been born-again, have you been saved?" With a handful of gospel tracts it is obvious to the young fans why I have come. I do not approach with a condemning attitude, but with a humble spirit to share the love of Jesus.

The students are hyped with a spirit of partying and revelry in anticipation of the game. As I walk down the rows of parked cars, peer group after peer group are guzzling beer to the pounding noise of music. The laughter is great and the spirits are carefree. They build waist high monuments of discarded beer cans and liquor bottles (they are not even old enough to legally purchase it) as if in competition with other social groups, as to who is having the most fun. The guys and girls teasingly grope one another as if sampling finger foods of carnal euphoria.

I am always amazed at how many young people tell me they have already been saved. Some are two beers tipsy and others are ten beers drunk. In order not to offend or be confrontational, I rejoice with them and move on to the next peer group looking for the individual who answers the question, "No, but I have been thinking about being saved."

However... many want to talk about the Bible, ask questions or make comments. These conversations have led me to form some opinions about the preaching from our pulpits over the past few years. These students are genuinely sincere when they tell me they have already been saved. They even rehearse for me, when they went down the aisle to ask Jesus to be their Savior. As evangelical preachers, we have done a wonderful job getting people to pray a prayer and confess Christ as Savior. In fact, statistically, ninety plus percent of Americans say they believe in God and most of them say they believe in Jesus Christ.

But is salvation a mere prayer to ask Jesus to save you from a burning hell? Everybody wants that. The Bible speaks of Christ's judgment when Jesus says, "Not everyone who says to Me, 'Lord, Lord,' shall enter the kingdom of heaven, but he who does the will of My Father in heaven. Many will say unto Me in that day, 'Lord, Lord, have we not prophesied [spoken] in Your name'...And I will declare unto them, 'I never knew you; depart from Me, you who practice lawlessness!'"[15] Obviously, salvation is more than a prayer of mere words.

> *Is salvation a mere prayer asking Jesus to save you from a burning hell?*

Note: Jesus said lordship means doing the will of God. Jesus did not deny being their Savior. He denied knowing them in a relationship of lordship.

I shudder at the thought of this crowd's "feast to the Lord." It is obvious they do not understand true salvation. The Apostle Peter talked about the Christian's repentant lifestyle. He said, "Since Christ suffered for us in the flesh, arm yourself with the same mind, for he who has suffered in the flesh has ceased from sin, that he no longer should live the rest of his time in the flesh for the lusts of men, but for the will of God. For we have spent enough of our past lifetime in doing the will of the Gentiles when we walked in lewdness, lusts, drunkenness, revelries, drinking parties, and abominable idolatries. In regard to these, they think it strange that you do not run with them in the same flood of dissipation, speaking evil of you."[16] These so called Christians are like the backslidden Hebrew worshipping the golden calf; they have believed *"the lie"* and deceived themselves.

This same crowd is poised and ready to embrace the microchip identity. They are so concerned with being accepted by the crowd, that the blind will follow the blind until they both fall into a ditch. They are really worshipping the spirit of the golden calf.

Parallel Four: God Gave Them Up

The Lord was angry at the backslidden Hebrew for worshipping the golden calf. His initial thought was to consume them, but because of Moses' intercession, he relented with mercy. In the end God pronounced judgment, "Whoever has sinned against Me, I will blot

him out of My book."[17] Stephen said in the New
Testament, "God gave them up to worship the host of
heaven." What do these two phrases, "I will blot you out"
and "God gave them up," mean?

When people anger the Lord by worshipping the
creature, God is a gentleman. He will not force Himself
on anyone. He created us for a love relationship and if we
refuse, though it grieves God's heart, He will let go.
Hence "God gave them up." What is the extent of
depravity that men will go to, without God's guidance in
their lives? They worshipped the host of heaven.

Stephen said the backslidden Hebrew went after the
god, Moloch. "The usual description given of this god is
that of a hollow image made of brass, having a human
body with the head of an ox [note: more cow worship].
The idol sat on a brazen throne with hands extended. In
sacrificing to it, the image was heated to redness by a fire
built within. The worshippers then placed their infant
children in the heated arms, while the noise of drums and
cymbals drowned the cries of the little sufferers."[18]

If a young couple went to a temple and did such a
thing today, they would be prosecuted to the fullest extent
of the law. They would be outcast from society and
possibly sentenced to death for the despicable act and the
temple would be shut down. Yet spiritual blindness has
deceived our society. A young couple can go into a clinic
and have the uterus inserted with a tube for the purpose of
sucking out their infant child. The young couple will be
applauded for their responsible behavior in saving the
community from an unwanted child. Even worse, the
government subsidizes clinics to encourage this practice
and when it is done, protects the young couple with their
laws. This worship of convenience and pleasure is as
hollow, as the ox-god Moloch.

The grieving spirit of God can be heard in the prophet's voice, "They set their abominations in the house which is called by My name, to defile it. 'And they built the high places of Baal [bull idol] which are in the Valley of the Son of Hinnom, to cause their sons and their daughters to pass through the fire to Molech, which I did not command them, nor did it come into My mind that they should do this...sin.'"[19] Even God who is all knowing said He could never have imagined how evil men could be and yet do it in His name and house.

Because the Hebrew "exchanged the truth of God for a lie, and worshiped and served the creature, more than the Creator", the Apostle Paul said, "For this reason God gave them up to vile passions. For even their women exchanged the natural use for what is against nature. Likewise also the men, leaving the natural use of the woman, burned in their lust for one another, men with men committing what is shameful, and receiving in themselves the penalty of their error which was due."[20]

God in His love for mankind, forewarned men not to lie with each other, because creation and life does not work this way.[21] God should know; He created life. The heart of God rends, each time an innocent person is affected with AIDS from a blood transfusion, or a child is born from infected parents. But God is a gentleman; He will not force Himself upon creation. He patiently ponders, how deep into sin will men go before they realize their need for God?

Stephen said, "God gave them up" to freely sin and that sin eventually weakened the Hebrew until they went into Babylonian captivity. Their slavery began long before they ever reached the land of Babylon. Paul said, "You are that one's slave whom you obey...of sin leading to death."[22]

As a pastor, I have had homeless drunks weep and sob on my shoulder begging me to help them. I have wept with friends who slowly wasted away with AIDS and consoled murderers in prison with life sentences. I am sorry, but I cannot help you. I would to God I could have taken away the craving for alcohol, perverted sex, and violence. But I cannot, only God can set men free. My compassion is merely a sample of God's mercy that men must partake of through repentance, *before* their sin leads them to bondage.

Golden calf worshippers waste away in spiritual dungeons long before they come to their prisons. They are so weakened by sin they cannot seem to muster the faith to repent of "sin leading to death." For only genuine repentance can bring them to the grace of God. I cannot repent for you, only you can repent of covetousness.

> *Golden Calf Worshippers waste away in spiritual dungeons long before they come to their prisons*

The golden calf is an evil deception. Its worship will cloud the judgment of men until sin comes to its culmination. Golden calf worshippers are weak in faith and will accept the microchip identity. They will be confident their decision is a good one. After all, they are following the crowd and everyone will be getting the implant.

Moses warned of deception. Deception means you are wrong, but you think you are right. Moses remarked of the deceived man, "He blesses himself in his heart, saying 'I shall have peace, even though I follow the dictates of my heart' as though the drunkard could be included with the sober…and the Lord [will] blot out his name from under heaven."[23]

Please remember the consequences of being a golden calf worshipper who receives the microchip identity. The Apostle John forewarn, "If anyone...receives his mark...He shall be tormented with fire and brimstone...and the smoke of their torment ascends forever and ever; and they have no rest day or night...whoever receives the mark...Here is the patience of the saints; here are those who keep the commandments of God and the faith of Jesus."[24]

God said, "I will blot you out." To be sent to hell is to have one's name blotted out from under heaven. The New Testament Greek word for hell comes from the Old Testament name Hinnom. The Valley of Hinnom is where the worshippers of the ox-god Molech cast out their dead babies. God's mind could not conceive of how far men could sink into sin's depravity. But when He saw the atrocities of His own people killing their children, He decided to create hell and let them reap what they had sown.

God's Mercy

The Psalmist said, "They made a calf in Horeb, and worshipped the molded image. Thus they changed their glory into the image of an ox that eats grass. They forgot God their Savior...Therefore He said that He would destroy them, had not Moses His chosen one stood before Him in the breach, to turn away His wrath, lest He destroy them."[25] Like Moses, Jesus is praying for those who have slipped into worshipping the golden calf. Jesus loves you. The Apostle Peter says, "The Lord...is longsuffering toward us, not willing that any should perish, but that all should come to repentance."[26]

Repentance is the key. Repentance is the voluntary decision to follow God, because God is good. The Psalmist wrote, "I will praise You, for I am fearfully and wonderfully made...When I was made in secret...Your eyes saw my substance, being yet unformed. And in Your book they all were written, the days fashioned for me, when as yet there were none of them. How precious also are Your thoughts to me, O God! How great is the sum of them! If I should count them, they would be more in number than the sand."[27] You are unique. God made you for this very hour, for noble purposes. He has "chosen you for himself, a special treasure above all the people of the earth."

Summary

When Israel rebelled against God, they made a golden calf and declared the image to be God. The carnality of Israel's golden calf is the same spirit today, as America embraces the microchip identity.

It is time to repent of golden calf worship, which is the love of money and materialism. Repentance will bring you into God's plan for your life. That plan is to be a conqueror over sin, and overcoming the microchip identity by trusting God.

Eight

Solomon's Double Life

"A house divided...falls." Luke 11:17

The management of a golf course cut expenses by hiring a novice ground's keeper. Management instructed the employee to sow seed on the putting greens. The novice mistakenly sowed seed on the greens that was meant for the fairways. The grass that grew was not the short Bermuda grass that allowed the ball to roll effortlessly across its manicured surface. Instead, stout blades of fescue mingled with the short Bermuda grass. Yes, the greens could be cut, but the stubborn fescue altered the path of the golf balls to the hole. Golfers soon turned to other courses in search of purer greens. Management paid a heavy price for their slothful hiring of the novice ground's keeper.

In the book of Genesis, there is a creation principle that is true in the natural as well as the spiritual. God said, "Let the earth bring forth grass, the herb that yields seed, and the fruit tree that yields fruit according to its kind, whose seed is in itself, on the earth."[1] The principle is simple. Whatever result you desire will be determined by the seed you sow. The Apostle Paul applied the idea to the spiritual realm when he wrote, "Do not be deceived, God is not mocked; for whatever a man sows, that he will also reap. For he who sows to his flesh will of the flesh reap corruption, but he who sows to the Spirit will of the Spirit reap everlasting life."[2]

How does this apply? The principle works in individuals as well as nations. People struggle within themselves to choose God over the flesh. This truth is evidenced in the life of Solomon who eventually forsook the Lord and, as a result, split the nation of Israel. Those two halves separated into those who worshipped the golden calf (Israel) and those who worshipped God (Judah).

Solomon's Double Life

> *Solomon spent his first twenty years building the house of God. His latter twenty years were spent pursuing carnality*

In order to understand the influence of the golden calf in the nation of Israel, we must first look at the double life of Solomon. King Solomon reigned for forty years. He spent his first twenty years building the house of God. His latter twenty years were spent pursuing carnality. Those carnal years laid the foundation for the restoration of the golden calf, whose worship had laid dormant for hundreds of years.

The culmination of Solomon's obedience came during the dedication of the newly built temple. The Bible records, "When Solomon finished praying, fire came down from heaven and consumed the burnt offering...and the glory of the Lord filled the temple."[3] It must have been an exciting moment to see the fire of God fall from heaven. After years of diligent planning and hard work, the dream of his father David was complete. God even made a promise, "I have heard your prayer...When I shut up heaven and there is no rain, or command the locust to devour the land, or send pestilence among my people, If My people who are called by My name will humble themselves, and pray and seek My face, and turn from their wicked ways, then I will hear from heaven, and will forgive their sin and heal their land."[4] This promise is important to the body of Christ. We will draw upon this promise in Part III as we seek revival and the return of America from the worship of the golden calf.

God also gave Solomon a stern warning, "But if you turn away...and go and serve other gods, and worship them, 'then I will uproot them from My land which I have given them; and this house which I have sanctified for My name I will cast out of My sight and will make it a proverb and a byword among all peoples.'"[5]

If there were ever a man born with the proverbial silver spoon in his mouth, it was Solomon. His father David had subdued the nation's enemies and appointed his son as king over the land. There was peace on every border.

> *"To whom much is given, from him much is required"*

Solomon had a godly father with a righteous upbringing and built God's house without distraction as he reigned over the land. But these blessings brought responsibility. The Scripture says, "To whom much is given, from him much is required."[6]

God required much, because Solomon was given much. Solomon's appetite for carnality in his latter years revived the spirit of the golden calf. That carnal spirit divided the nation of Israel and resulted in ten tribes worshipping the golden calf. The golden calf worship led to the uprooting of the people from the land, just as God had promised. But it was the carnal spirit of Solomon that caused Israel to return to golden calf worship. The carnal seeds that revived golden calf worship can be seen in Solomon's lifestyle.

Solomon's carnal seasons can be summed up in this verse. God commanded the Israelites, "When you...say, 'I will set a king over me like all the nations that are around me,' ...he shall not multiply horses for himself...neither shall he multiply wives for himself...nor shall he greatly multiply silver and gold for himself."[7] This commandment regarding the king was totally ignored by Solomon. He multiplied wives, horses, silver and gold.

Women

A Hebrew historian writes, "King Solomon loved many foreign women...from the nations of whom the Lord had said...You shall not intermarry with them...Surely they will turn away your hearts after their gods. Solomon clung to these in love. And he had seven hundred wives, princesses, and three hundred concubines; and his wives turned away his heart. For it was so, when Solomon was old, that his wives turned his heart after other gods; and his heart was not loyal to the Lord his God...Solomon did evil...[and] built a high place for Chemosh the abomination of Moab...and for [the ox-god] Molech...And he did likewise for all his foreign wives, who burned incense and sacrificed to their gods. So the Lord became angry with Solomon...Therefore the Lord said to Solomon...I will tear the kingdom away from you...Nevertheless, I will not do it in your days, for the sake of your father David; I will tear it out of the hand of your son."[8]

Solomon could not possibly satisfy all these women physically or emotionally. Simple math reveals he could spend only one day of undivided attention every two years and eight months, with each of his wives and concubines.

The spirit of golden calf worship is the same today. Many men who claim the name of Christ pursue multiple sexual relationships. They are caught up in the sensuality of beauty and flirting instead of pursuing a monogamous marriage with a godly woman. They can never seem to be satisfied physically or emotionally as they go from relationship to relationship. Their lust for women saps them of their time, money and focus, drawing them away from fulfilling their call in Christ to be a unique and special people.

The prophet Nehemiah noted the magnitude of sensual women, "Did not Solomon king of Israel sin by these things? Yet among many nations there was no king like him, who was beloved of his God...Nevertheless pagan women caused even him to sin. Should we then hear of your doing all this great evil, transgressing against our God by marrying pagan women?"[9] The Christian must repent and pursue sexual purity and choose a spouse who loves the Lord.

Horses

The Scriptures tell us, "Solomon had horses imported from Egypt..."[10] and "Solomon had forty thousand stalls of horses for his chariots...."[11] Horses had a couple of uses. First they were for military enhancement. Secondly, they were for transportation.

King David, the father of Solomon said, "Some trust in chariots, and some in horses; But we will remember the name of the Lord our God."[12] David further explained, "No king is saved by the multitude of an army; A mighty man is not delivered by great strength. A horse is a vain hope for safety; Neither shall it deliver any by its great strength."[13] David was simply saying that trust in God should be first and foremost. As Solomon's love waned for God, he multiplied horses to insure military might.

As a nation, we should maintain the finest military in the world. But we should not lean on military might for our safety alone. As a Christian nation, we should be diligent in worship of Christ. To relax in Christian piety while trusting in cruise missiles and F-16 fighter jets is holding to a form of godliness, but denying the power thereof.

The second use of horses was for transportation with chariots. The noble and the mighty enjoyed this mode of travel. Today, I cannot help but ponder America's pursuit of cars. But not just any car, it seems we must have the very latest and greatest technology with all the bells and whistles. Without question, men are making a statement about their wealth and affluence with their cars. Americans love pleasure and convenience, but no amount of engineering can replace true Christian character. "Man looks at the outward appearance, but the Lord looks at the heart."[14] If you as a Christian are driving the best money can buy but are not honoring the Lord in financial giving, like it or not you have slipped into worshipping the golden calf.

Silver and Gold

Solomon had a carnal appetite for silver and gold. The Scriptures note, "The weight of gold that came to

Solomon yearly was six hundred and sixty-six talents of gold...All King's Solomon's drinking vessels were gold...Not one was silver, for this was counted as nothing in the days of Solomon...The king made silver as common in Jerusalem as stones...."[15] The Holy Spirit inspired the writer to note the quantity of gold. The number 666 is the same number of the Anti-Christ. The number is a reflection of the culmination of man's ingenuity, which is also expressed in the microchip identity. Can you grasp the massive wealth that existed in Solomon's day? I can hardly fathom silver as abundant as gravel.

Today the spirit is the same. We hold our consumer economy as sacred. The pursuit of money is paramount in American society. Men revolve their lives around jobs and paychecks. They work from sun up to sun down to the demise of their families, health and church attendance. The lack of self-control with credit cards destroys the marriage union as men become slaves to debt. The pursuit of money and the microchip identity are evidence of a society that is caught up in the worship of the golden calf.

Pride

When a man's affluence yields money, women and materialism, he gets lifted up with pride. Solomon's arrogance prompted him to do an unusual thing. The Scriptures declared, "Moreover the king made a great throne of ivory, and overlaid it with pure gold. The throne had six steps...Twelve lions stood there, one on each side of the six steps; nothing like this had been made for any other kingdom."[16]

Solomon ruled the known world of his time. The design of his unique throne speaks volumes about the backslidden, self-centered attitude of Solomon. Approaching the throne for judgment, the base of the chair was positioned so the individual would be looking at the feet of the sitting king. As the commoner's eyes scanned the throne from left to right, he would see six lions, six steps and six more lions. The gold plated throne was designed to elevate the king's preeminence in trepidation over the awe struck peasant. The symbolism of 666 should be a reminder to every man of the end result of following carnal appetites, for the number of the Anti-Christ is the 666.

> *As the commoner's eyes scanned the throne from left to right, he would see six lions, six steps and six more lions*

Solomon's carnal season paints a picture of these last days. When mankind lusts for money, women and materialism, the spiritual atmosphere is ripe for restoring the worship of the golden calf.

God's Will For Solomon

God's will for Solomon is the same for all Christians, for Jesus "has made us kings to His God."[17] When God gave instructions to the king not to multiply "wives, horses, silver and gold", He also instructed what the king should do. God said, "When he sits on the throne of his kingdom, that he shall write for himself a copy of this law in a book, from the one before the priests...he shall read it all the days of his life, that he may learn to fear [reverence] the Lord his God and be careful to observe all the words...that his heart may not be lifted above his brethren, that he may not turn aside from the commandment...that he may prolong his days in his kingdom, he and his children in the midst of Israel."[18] These commandments of God ensured freedom and continued revival for the land. As Christians, we must observe five truths within this command.

One: A Copy for Himself

As a king, you must make the Word of God your own. You must receive God's instructions as personal. So often, people view church from a distance. Often they come for the social gathering or just for the excitement of the worship, preaching or program. They see and hear, but never really come to a personal change. Somehow, they separate the Bible as something that preachers and religious people do and never see the Scriptures as God's personal message to them.

Many people treat the Bible like the "crown jewels" of England. They pass by the crown's display case, dreaming of what it must have been to be a king and to possess such jewels. As they exit the museum, they remember they are tourists and not royalty, and the memory of wearing the crown soon fades. But the Bible says, "For God so loved the world that He gave His only begotten Son, that whosoever believes in Him should not perish but have everlasting life."[19] God loves you. He longs for you to know Him and follow His ways so you will have life. He desires for you to walk as a king, reigning in life.

Two: Read Everyday

As a king, you are instructed to read everyday. It is human nature to forget. This is why King David wrote, "Bless the Lord, O my soul, and forget not all His benefits: ...Who *crowns* you with lovingkindness and tender mercies, Who satisfies your mouth with good things...."[20]

My family has a yearly tradition at Christmas. We have a blank book with the above Scripture written in the front. Year after year, we gather together in front of the fireplace on Christmas Eve and reflect on the past twelve months, writing down the benefits of the Lord. We remember individual blessings and write them into the pages dated for that year.

One fascinating aspect of this special evening is reading the entries of previous years. We read of answered prayers for healings, salvations and financial blessings. The faces of each family member rejoice with glee as we remember, because we have forgotten. This is the reason for the book and the tradition, so we *will* remember.

Personally, I am most vulnerable to carnal appetites when I get discourage or depressed. It is in these low moments that I wrestle with temptation and wonder if God even cares. But I have discovered a regular routine of reading the Bible reminds me of God's goodness. Reading helps me remember God's benefits and keeps my priorities straight. Those priorities help me to behave in a manner worthy of a king.

Three: Observe and Do

The tabloids are notorious for selling papers extolling the carnality of royalty. Why? The tabloids know people will pay to read about the latest affair of the princess and/or her evening of drunkenness. Knowing the shortcomings of royalty seems to comfort people. The infatuation seems to reassure people that kings and queens are really just like them. It's true, "God is no respecter of persons."[21] Titles and bloodlines of ancestry mean nothing to God. No amount of royal clothing, jewelry or castles can deliver an individual from the misery of life if they pursue carnality. The royal mess of royal lives is proof enough.

The Apostle Paul called into question the validity of a Hebrew being God's child for ancestry alone. He said, "For he is not a Jew who is one outwardly...but he is a Jew who is one inwardly; and circumcision is that of the heart, in the Spirit..."[22] Paul further stated, "They are not all Israel who are of Israel, nor are they all children because they are the seed of Abraham..."[23] He is simply saying that God is looking for those who will follow the Spirit of the Lord. It does not matter what nation, family, social strata or religious denomination you were born into, for "Whoever calls on the name of the Lord shall be saved."[24]

Living like a king is available to all who follow Jesus. Nobility is not about ancestry, castles or clothing. Nobility is about character. Jesus describes the relationship we can have with God. "If anyone loves Me, he will keep My word; and My Father will love him, and We will come to him and make Our home with him." [25] To be clothed in the character of obedience is the reflection

> *Living like a king is available to all who follow Jesus. Nobility is not about ancestry, castles or clothing. Nobility is about character*

of God. When we obey God, we become part of His home. That means His Spirit is dwelling in us and we in Him, resulting in peace and joy. This is freedom. This is liberty. This is kingdom living.

Four: Do Not Turn Aside

Royalty and loyalty, go hand in hand. Solomon's double life exposed his disloyalty. He knew the commandments of God and ignored them. This was not a sin of ignorance, but of rebellion. Solomon admitted, "I set my heart to know madness and folly."[26] He further stated, "I also gathered for myself silver and gold and the special treasures of kings...Whatever my eyes desired I did not keep from them. I did not withhold my heart from any pleasure...and indeed all was vanity and grasping for the wind. There was no profit under the sun."[27]

> *Royalty and Loyalty go hand in hand*

The carnal king's behavior is the same today. People live for the moment, for pleasure, for the lusts of their flesh. "Eat drink and be merry," they say, "for tomorrow we die." It's as if there is no afterlife or judgment. Therefore they must get the most out of life, for they only live once. God forewarned of this turning aside, "lest your heart be lifted up with pride." The pursuit of such worldliness blinds one's soul and leads them into the bondage of the golden calf, which is vanity and grasping at the wind.

Godly wisdom says, "It is not for kings to drink wine, nor for princes intoxicating drink; lest they drink and forget the law and pervert the justice of the afflicted."[28] Righteous kings are loyal to the one who appointed them. They understand their responsibility to the kingdom and to serve the best interest of the people. Godly kings discipline themselves to their royal calling and avoid turning aside.

True Christians recognize the importance of loyalty. Consider the relevance of this Scripture, "Let us hold fast the confession of our hope without wavering...and let us consider one another in order to stir up love and good works, not forsaking the assembling of ourselves together, as is the manner of some, but exhorting one another, and so much the more as you see the [judgment] Day approaching. For if we sin willfully after we have received the knowledge of the truth, there no longer remains a sacrifice for sins, but a certain fearful expectation of judgment..."[29] Faithful church attendance with the idea of encouraging others in the kingdom develops the royal attribute of loyalty.

Five: Prolong Days

A king's behavior yields consequences both good and bad. As the king goes, so go the people with regard to their behavior. Solomon indeed had a certain expectation of God's judgment, as he anticipated the rending of the kingdom from his son. This rending took place because the selfish seeds of carnality germinated in the hearts of the people, and many departed from the temple of God. As a result, the kingdom was divided.

A righteous king understands the influence he has. When he uses his influence wisely, he imparts life to others. But when he is corrupt, he destroys others. Have you ever heard someone say, "Well it is my life, I can do what I want"! Actually, the life is not his. It belongs to God who will hold him accountable for how he lives. Jesus declared, "A good man out of the good treasure of his heart brings forth good things, and an evil man out of the evil treasure brings forth evil things. But I

> *A righteous king understands the influence he has. When he uses his influence wisely, he imparts life to others. But when he is corrupt, he destroys others.*

say to you that for every idle word men may speak, they will give account of it in the Day of Judgment."[30]

When I was twelve years old, my parents relocated to a different city for one year. In my earnestness to make new friends, I fell into the wrong crowd. My bad behavior got me into a lot of trouble and corrupted others. But my worst memory came years later, after I had turned to the Lord with repentance. While living at college, an old acquaintance from that city invited me out for a cup of coffee. As we reminisced, it became apparent that he had picked up my carnal ways. My childhood friend was a mirror of my former carnality and the sway I had in his life. I was ashamed of the fruit of my influence. I determined to change, and because of Christ, I want to influence others for good, not evil.

Royalty seeks to serve, not to be served. Jesus demonstrated this attitude when He came to lay down His life for many.

The Nation Hung in the Balance

Solomon repented in his latter years. He came to his senses and realized carnality had achieved nothing but vanity. At the end of his life he wrote, "Let us hear the conclusion of the whole matter: Fear God and keep His commandments, for this is man's all. For God will bring every work into judgment...."[31] Unfortunately, the damage was done. The kingdom split as God promised, and the carnal spirit of Solomon resurrected the worship of the golden calf.

Summary

The spiritual state of America is much like Solomon. Our fathers fought wars and defeated our enemies. Our country has known extremely prosperous economic times. Peace has allowed us the opportunity to build God's house, and we have a Christian heritage

> *Like Solomon, the "me generation" has been sidetracked by carnality and has laid the foundation for The Last Golden Calf.*

from our forefathers. But many have chosen to ignore God's commands and instead pursue money, women and materialism. Like Solomon, the "me generation" has been sidetracked by carnality and has laid the foundation for *The Last Golden Calf*.

In the next chapter, we will see how many in Israel chose the way of the golden calf and were destroyed. As Christians we must learn from the mistakes of Solomon's double life. As kings before God, our destiny is not to fall, but to serve our nation with the example of Christ's character. We must repent of our carnal man and remember the promise God made, "If My people who are called by My name will humble themselves, and pray and seek My face, and turn from their wicked ways, then I will hear from heaven, and will forgive their sin and heal their land."[32] It is not too late. Let us turn from our materialistic ways and draw others to God.

Nine

The Divided Kingdom

"Jeroboam...made two calves of gold...
devised in his own heart...." 1 Kings 12:28, 33

Rehoboam became king after his father Solomon died. Because of Solomon's harsh governing style, the people yearned for relief. When King Rehoboam refused to lighten the oppression, the people made Jeroboam king over ten tribes in Israel. Thus, God split the kingdom because of Solomon's evil pursuits, just as God had promised.[1]

Because the people went to Jerusalem three times a year to celebrate the feasts of the Lord, King Jeroboam realized the people's allegiance might return to King Rehoboam of Judah. "Therefore the king asked advice, made two calves of gold, and said to the people, 'It is too much for you to go up to Jerusalem. Here are your gods, O Israel, which brought you up from the land of Egypt!'"[2]

Certainly the people knew their national history. Most assuredly their forefathers told the stories of Moses parting the Red Sea and their deliverance from Egypt. They definitely had learned of the wilderness journey and the lesson about God's judgment for the golden calf, for it was written in their law. And yet, people who were called by God's name still followed Jeroboam to worship the golden calves. How can it be? Does this make any sense? Yes, it is perfectly logical when you consider the power of covetousness.

The Power of Covetousness

The spirit of lust or covetousness brings people to a place of irrational behavior. The drug addict knows the heroin might kill him, but injects the needle anyway. The young teenager learns sex education in school, but still crawls into the back seat of a car and risks pregnancy. And the shoplifter ignores the thought that he might suffer shame in getting caught. Yes, lust, greed and covetousness blind the heart to senseless behavior.

The Israelites so coveted Solomon's lavish lifestyle of the past twenty years, they were now willing to worship a cow as their source of sustenance. Because the nations of the world worshipped cows, it was easy to justify. The covetous example of Solomon had conditioned their hearts. They were tired of serving a king who enjoyed all the benefits. They too wanted the women, horses, silver and gold. After all, their nation was the greatest society known to man and they should have it all.

The story of Jeroboam's golden calves is told in the Old Testament chapters of 1 Kings 12-14 and 2 Chronicles 10-12. It is a lesson that teaches about a nation's propensity to stray from the path of God. America has heard the Sunday School stories about God and judgment. Yet, like the Israelites, many are succumbing to the power of covetousness to accept the microchip identity.

When in history has man ever bought and sold with anything but money or barter? God foretold that man would buy and sell with a mark in their right hands or foreheads, just before the return of Jesus Christ. The microchip identity should awaken everyone; now is the time to honor God, not the golden calf.

Jeroboam utilized the spirit of covetousness to turn the people away from God with his golden calves. The Anti-Christ's microchip identity will do the same. The story of Jereboam's golden calves has several dynamics that are parallel to these last days. Let us observe the similarities between the golden calves of Jeroboam and the microchip identity of the Anti-Christ.

Similarity One: Raised Up By God

God raised up Jeroboam[3] and in the days to come, God will raise up the Anti-Christ. Just as God gave Jeroboam ten tribes, God gives the Anti-Christ ten kingdoms. Consider this Scripture, "For God has put it into their hearts to fulfill His purpose, to be of one mind, and to give their kingdom to the beast, until the words of God are fulfilled."[4] This is God's doing. It is God's plan to allow men to choose whom they will follow. God is dividing the allegiance of men between those who will follow the golden calf and those who will follow God.

This world-wide microchip identity is what Jesus was referring to when He spoke of, "The hour of trial which shall come upon the whole world, to test those who dwell on the earth."[5]

> *"The hour of trial which shall come upon the whole world to test those who dwell on the earth" - Jesus*

Similarity Two: Political Strife

"The similarity of the names Jeroboam and Rehoboam may indicate that both names were given when the two kings ascended their thrones, a common custom. Both names stress the power of the people."[7] Jeroboam's name means, "May the people be great" and Rehoboam's name means, "May the people increase."[8] The names are a reflection of their governing attitudes.

Jeroboam wanted less government. He believed the people were great and wanted less bureaucratic oppression. Rehoboam wanted more government. As the people increased, he believed they needed more laws and more bureaucratic oversight. Does this sound like Republicans and Democrats? Amazingly, it's the same political climate as today.

I know many Christian Republicans who are sick and tired of taxation, government interference and the immoral stance of pro-choice Democrats. I also know many Christian Democrats who are fed up with the wealthy elite who want to share less and less with the unfortunate. God is not a Republican or a Democrat.

It does not seem to matter what party is in office, either way the microchip identity is coming like a freight train at a railroad crossing. It does not matter what side of the track you entered from, the devil's plan is to keep you sidetracked with political squabbling until all are crushed. Christians are sometimes more concerned with their party being in power than with God. What Christians need is genuine revival. When God is Lord, people walk in morality, giving to one another and are at peace with one another. Christians do not need a world system; they need God's Spirit.

Similarity Three: "Devised in his own heart"

The Bible says of golden calf religion, "Jeroboam ordained a feast...like the feast that was in Judah...sacrificing to the calves that he had made...which he had devised in his own heart."[9] This bogus worship was man-made. Today's counterfeit religion is all about pleasure and recreation. Have you ever noticed a concert resembles a worship service? The masses lift their hands in adoration of the lead singer, reciting lyrics about wine, women, money, and having a good time. The people shout as the lyrical guru affirms their chosen lifestyle.

The Apostle Paul said, "In the last days perilous times will come: for men will be lovers of themselves, lovers of money...lovers of pleasure rather than lovers of God, having the form of godliness but denying its power. And from such people turn away!"[10]

People seem to think that beautiful homes, cars and clothing are a reflection of basic goodness. It is true that good morals will lead to prosperity. However, if one's lifestyle is void of a personal relationship with Jesus Christ, his possessions really express pride, selfishness and covetousness. God exhorts us to turn away from such, lest we get caught up in the same spirit and embrace the microchip identity.

Similarity Four: "Rejected True Priests"

The Bible says, "The Levites...came to Judah and Jerusalem, for Jeroboam and his sons had rejected them from serving as priests to the Lord. Then he appointed for himself priests for the high places, for demons, and the calf idols, which he had made. And after the Levites left, those from all the tribes of Israel, such as set their heart to seek the Lord God of Israel, came to Jerusalem to sacrifice to the Lord God of their fathers."[11]

They do not celebrate Christmas, Easter or Thanksgiving. They celebrate Santa, the bunny and turkey day

The spirit is the same today. The golden calf crowd worships their careers as their source, not God. Often, they hardly even know a preacher. They do not read the Bible. The Christians they do know, they write off as being irrelevant in the twenty-first century and pat themselves on the back for being tolerant of them. They do not celebrate Christmas, Easter or Thanksgiving. They celebrate Santa, the bunny and turkey day.

At my son's college graduation, I was appalled to witness no affirmations of God. No invocation or benediction prayers were offered, just pep talks by various alumni on how to be successful and change the world for a better place. Thirty years ago, it was commonplace to begin public events with prayer. If the secular university allowed prayer today, the golden calf crowd that rejected the true priests might sue.

The golden calf divided the nation of Israel between the carnal and the spiritual. Those who set their hearts to seek the Lord came to Jerusalem. They understood the golden calf sham and rejected its phoniness. Likewise today, it is time for genuine lovers of God to return to church and worship God.

Similarity Five: "It's Too Much Trouble"

Jeroboam set up the golden calves and declared, "It is too much for you to go up to Jerusalem."[12] Golden calf worshippers see church as burdensome. They would rather sleep in on Sunday morning. Church is an inconvenience. If they do go, they sulk as they count the seconds away looking at their watches.

"Oh, what a weariness"[13], says the golden calf crowd. They do not even realize the subtle spirit motivating them to make excuses. They always have something better to do, the beach, the park, a picnic, a ballgame, something, anything, but church. There are 168 hours in the week and they cannot give one hour to say "thank you" to the Creator of the universe. They sigh, "I do not have time." But in reality, they have the same 24 hours everyman has; what they do not have is priority for God. All of their time is spent pursuing the golden calf.

God is dividing out the golden calf followers. This spirit of weariness is a sure sign of deep spiritual trouble. The Scriptures say, "For the message of the cross is foolishness to those who are perishing."[14] If you identify with this spirit, it is time to seek God for a real experience with the Holy Spirit. I exhort you to find out why genuine Christians are excited about Jesus.

Similarity Six: Avoid the Feasts in Jerusalem

Jeroboam gave a reason for the golden calves. "If these people go up to offer sacrifices in the house of the Lord at Jerusalem, then the heart of this people will turn back to their lord...."[15] The Hebrew attended three festivals a year in Jerusalem. The celebrations were designed to remind them of the goodness of God. Jeroboam and the Anti-Christ want the golden calf crowd to remain ignorant of these kindnesses shown in these three festivals.

The Feast of Passover celebrated God's deliverance, when the death angel slew all the firstborn children of

Egypt. The Hebrew were instructed by God to eat a lamb and strike the doorposts of their homes with its blood. When the death angel saw the blood of the lamb, he by-passed the firstborn children of the Hebrew, but slew the firstborn of the Egyptians, proving the judgment was from the hand of God.

The Scriptures say of Jesus, "Behold The Lamb of God who takes away the sin of the world!"[16] When God's eternal judgment comes, those who have been "born again" will be saved because they embraced Jesus the Lamb. All men have been born once in the flesh. But those who follow God have been born twice. Their hearts have changed from being followers of carnal appetites to being followers of God. Hence the phrase "born again" means born once in the flesh and second in the spirit. The Feast of Passover reflected the goodness of God to forgive those who had partaken of the lamb.

The second *Feast of Pentecost,* "Celebrated the revelation of God at Mount Sinai."[17] After Moses led them out of Egypt, the Israelites experienced the awesome power of God on the mountain. Imagine for a moment, feeling the thrill of God's presence. You can!

"How is it that You will manifest Yourself to us, and not to the world?"

The disciples of Jesus experienced the infilling of God's presence on the Day of Pentecost. Jesus said, "You shall receive power when the Holy Spirit has come upon you; and you shall be My witnesses...to the ends of the earth."[18] The Spirit fills the Christian with power. The Apostle Paul wrote, "For the kingdom of God is not eating and drinking, but righteousness and peace and joy in the Holy Spirit."[19] Golden calf worship is ignorant of this ability to experience the presence of God.

This explains why a disciple asked Jesus, "How is it that You will manifest Yourself to us, and not to the world?"[20] Like the disciple, if you seek God, you will experience God. Unfortunately, the golden calf crowd only knows eating and drinking.

The third *Feast of Tabernacles* celebrated God's provisions for the Hebrew during their forty-year journey through the wilderness to the promised land. Each year they would build temporary huts and live outdoors for seven days. This yearly event reminded them of the cloud that comforted from the desert sun, the fire that warm at night, the quail and manna that was given to eat, the rock that gave them water and their clothes and shoes that never wore out. The Hebrew did not have grocery stores to buy supplies, yet God provided for every need.

Jesus used miracles to provide for His followers. He multiplied fish and bread. He told Peter where to harvest a boatload of fish in return for allowing Him to preach from his boat. Jesus told Peter on another occasion to cast a line and catch a fish, which had a gold coin in its mouth to pay their taxes. These are miraculous provisions.

When the Anti-Christ mandates the microchip identity, he wants you to forget God's provisions. He wants you to believe the golden calf is your source, not God. But Jesus exhorted, "Do not worry, saying, 'What shall we eat?' or 'What shall we drink?' or 'What shall we wear?' For after all these things the Gentiles seek. For your heavenly Father knows that you need all these things. But seek first the kingdom of God and His righteousness, and all these things shall be added to you. Therefore do not worry about tomorrow...."[21] This promise does not become null and void during the mandatory season of the microchip identity. The promise becomes magnified.

It is God's goodness to save and provide. Jeroboam sought to rob the Hebrew of these festival truths. The golden calf crowd lost the understanding of these feasts because they avoided God's temple to pursue money, women, and materialism.

Similarity Seven: A Golden Calf in Dan

The Bible says of the golden calves, "And he [Jeroboam] set one up in Bethel and the other he put in Dan. Now this thing became a sin, for the people went to worship before the one as far as Dan."[22]   God's temple was in Jerusalem. A map of Israel locates the city of Dan on the border of Lebanon, as far north from Jerusalem as geographically possible. To travel to Dan was literally to go in the opposite direction of the will of God.

Why is the microchip identity directly opposed to the will of God? God's first two commandments were, "Thou shalt have no other gods before me" and "Thou shalt not make unto thee any graven image."[23] God wants mankind to follow His Spirit. Our faith is not in ceremony or religious artifacts. Jesus said, "The hour is coming, and now is, when the true worshipers will worship the Father in spirit and in truth; for the Father is seeking such to worship Him. God is Spirit, and those who worship Him must worship in spirit and truth."[24] Christians walk hand in hand with their Father's Spirit. It's a father-child communion. Christianity is not a religion; it is a living relationship with God through Jesus Christ.

The microchip identity violates both commandments. To receive the microchip is to acknowledge the Anti-Christ as your source or provider, and thus as your god. The Greek word for "mark", as in "mark of the beast" is "charagma." It literally means, "a scratch or etching such as a stamp or badge of servitude"[25] and comes from a root word meaning "to sharpen to a point with the idea of scratching."[26] The microchip itself is a graven image. It is made of silicone and engraved with circuitry. And to be inserted, a needle is required that scratches the skin.

In Biblical times, "slaves were branded with a peculiar mark to designate their master."[27] Today, cattle ranchers still signify ownership by branding their cows. To receive the identity chip or the "mark of the beast" is to acknowledge the Anti-Christ as your owner and master.

> *In Biblical times, "slaves were branded with a peculiar mark to designate their master."*

God's will is different. Jesus said, "He who overcomes…I will write on him the name of My God…I will write on him My new name."[28] Just as intimate couples give personal nicknames to each other, God gives His followers His name. Like an intimate password, it gives you access to the Creator of the universe.

Similarity Eight: A Golden Calf in Bethel

"[Jeroboam] made priests from every class of people, who were not of the sons of Levi…So he did at Bethel, sacrificing to the calves that he had made…which he had devised in his own heart."[29] Bethel is significant because the name means, "House of God."[30]

When Jacob was fleeing from his brother Esau, who wanted to kill him, he came to a city called Luz in Palestine. Luz means, "growing there."[31] There, Jacob had an encounter with God while sleeping. In his dream, he saw angels ascending and descending a ladder and then God appeared and gave this promise. "I am the Lord God…the land on which you lie I will give to you and your descendants…in your seed all the families of the earth shall be blessed. Behold I am with you and will keep you wherever you go…I will not leave you until I have done what I have spoken to you."[32]

Jacob was so awestruck by the encounter with God, he said, "Surely the Lord is in this place, and I did not know it…how awesome is this place! This is none other than the house of God…and he called the name of that place Bethel…"[33] Jacob interpreted God's promise in a very simple and practical way, as he made this vow. "If God will be with me, and keep me in this way that I am going, and give me bread to eat and clothing to put on, so that I come back to my father's house in peace, then the Lord shall be my God…and of all that You give me I will surely give a tenth to You."[34]

| *Bethel means "House Of God"* |

Everyone needs a Luz-Bethel encounter with God. Each man needs the confidence of knowing God is with him: that God will provide, protect and never leave you. Those who have this spiritual experience, freely give back to God. The tenth is a thanksgiving testimony of their confidence in God's provision.

The golden calf crowd turns away from trusting God. They substitute the golden calf for the house of God. They believe giving tithes is foolishness and a sure way to poverty. Their thanksgiving offerings are given to sports figures, movie stars, and super models. They are predisposed to follow the Anti-Christ.

It is important to seek God for the Luz-Bethel encounter. The confidence of God dwelling with you will keep you from living in fear and accepting the microchip identity.

Similarity Nine: Shishak and the Ark

Remaining in Judah and following King Rehoboam can also be dangerous. The Bible says, "It came to pass when Rehoboam had...strengthened himself, that he forsook the law of the Lord...and ...Shishak king of Egypt came up against Jerusalem, because they had transgressed against the Lord...and took away the treasures of the house of the Lord...."[35] Shishak was an ally to Jeroboam. Many archeologists believe Shishak took the Ark of the Covenant from the temple, which represented the presence of God, the greatest treasure of the Hebrew.

To attend church and listen to sermons, but not follow God's heart is to lose any sense of the presence of God. People mistakenly assume the title "Christian" for many reasons: adult or infant water baptism, confirmation, denominational membership, they said a salvation prayer, attend to religion ceremonies such as communion or even birth in a Christian nation.

The Bible repeatedly affirms this truth, "Do not merely listen to the word, and so deceive yourselves. Do what it says...the man who...continues to do this, not forgetting what he has heard, but doing it...he will be blessed in what he does."[36] Remember, God is not looking for people who will be religious, but people who will follow His heart.

From the time Solomon quit building the house of God and began pursuing carnality, it only took twenty-five years for Israel to lose their national treasure; the presence of God represented in the Ark. Israel was the greatest nation of its time, boasting a mighty army. And yet, the military was no match for the invading army of

Shishak. They had no inner strength, resolve, or character to resist.

Summary

The wickedness of Jeroboam's golden calves is evident. His name and sin is mentioned nearly twenty times in the Bible as future kings were said to have, "Walked in all the way of Jeroboam... and in the sins which he made Israel to sin."[37] Each king's generation continued the golden calf religion until it became an accepted way of life in the divided kingdom. God's purpose in Jeroboam and the last days' counter-part of the Anti-Christ is to force people to choose, thus dividing the kingdom between good and evil.

America is divided. It is wonderful to see many with bumper stickers and fish symbols proudly displaying the owner's confession of Jesus as Lord. But I grieve for the masses that have no concept of what is taking place in our nation's spirit. Slumping figures of church attendance shout loudly, "America, you are in deep spiritual trouble. You have lost your way."

To golden calf worshippers, "God bless America" means, "give me the blessings." They do not seek God; they seek God's hand. To them, America's freedom is all about money, prosperity and pleasure. The golden calf crowd has succumbed to worshipping the created thing more than the Creator of those things. This phony religion is dividing our nation.

Without repentance, the golden calf worshippers will be drawn to the microchip identity like moths to a bug light. They will be zapped into spiritual suicide because they loved pleasure more than God.

Ten

The Covetous Spirit

"Command those who are rich in this present age not to be haughty, nor to trust in uncertain riches but in the living God, who gives us richly all things to enjoy."
1 Timothy 6:17

I remember catching crawdads in the creek as a kid. After getting pinched by their claws I came up with a new plan. The strategy was deceptive. I simply used a twig in one hand to approach the miniature lobster and held a tin can to his backside with the other hand. As I slowly guided the twig towards the cautious crayfish, he would back right into the can. Once captured, the crawdads were boiled and served as appetizers to all my friends. The plan was simple, devious, and it worked.

Like catching crawdads, the devil has a simple, but devious plan in these last days. Because of terrorism, the masses are focused on "peace and safety." They fear the loss of their current way of life. That fear is drawing them into the deceptive tin can, the microchip identity. The microchip implant is supposed to bring security and economic freedom, but the masses are unaware that "sudden destruction is upon them"[1] with the loss of

salvation to all who receive the mark.[2] By keeping the
masses focused on earthly things, the devil steals their
souls as they declare their allegiance to the Anti-Christ.

The Bible speaks of numerous sins that will lead to
spiritual death. Consider this passage and take special
note of covetousness. "Do you not know that the
unrighteous will not inherit the kingdom of God? Do not
be deceived. Neither fornicators, nor idolaters, nor
adulterers, nor homosexuals, nor sodomites, nor thieves,
nor *covetous*, nor drunkards, nor revilers, nor extortioners
will inherit the kingdom of God."[3]

Defining Covetousness

Webster's dictionary defines *covet*: "to want ardently."
The Greek renderings of the biblical words *covetous* and
covetousness are; to fill or to fulfill like a flood. To hold
or desire more, and eager for gain.[4] The words have a
broad application. Covetous instances in the Bible are
varied; Eve desired the forbidden fruit from the tree of the
knowledge of good and evil, Laban defrauded Jacob of
his wages, Ahab yearned for Naboth's vineyard, while
David lusted for Bath-sheba and the rich young ruler
loved his money.[5] The covetous spirit pursues many
objects of affection; food, land, money, women, and
materialism.

Having a strong desire is not necessarily a bad thing.
God encourages, "Covet earnestly the best [spiritual]
gifts."[6] He wants us to be "special people, zealous of
good works." It is the desire for earthly possessions
elevated higher than our love for God that ruins our
spiritual relationship.

Let's look at three stories that portray men straying from the faith. Each is godly, yet errs from the faith because of the love of money.

Gehazi

Gehazi was the servant of Elisha and the story is told in 2 Kings 5:15-27. His master had performed a miracle in healing the leprosy of a Syrian named Naaman, who desired to show appreciation by giving a gift. Elisha refused declaring, "As the Lord lives, before whom I stand, I will receive nothing." However, Gehazi coveted the gift.

The servant waited until the Syrian had departed and then chased after him. Once in Naaman's presence, Gehazi misrepresented Elisha by saying, "My Master has sent me, saying...Please give...a talent of silver and two changes of garments." Of course the healed man gave abundantly to Gehazi all he requested and more.

When Gehazi returned, Elisha confronted the covetous servant, "Is it time to receive money and to receive clothing, olive groves and vineyards, sheep and oxen, male and female servants? Therefore

"Is it time to receive money and to receive clothing?"

the leprosy of Naaman shall cling to you and your descendants forever. And he went out from his presence leprous, as white as snow."

The lessons to be learned are these. First, there is a time to receive abundance, and there is a time to honor God by denying self. Obviously during the season of the microchip identity, it will be a time to honor God, not to covet abundance. Secondly, the spirit of covetousness was symbolized by leprosy. Leprosy always forced men to live away from the family of God.

Balaam

The story of the seer Balaam is told in Numbers 22. Balaam lived along the way as the Israelites were going to the promised land. King Balak of Moab requested the prophet curse them, because he had heard of their mighty miracles as they came from Egypt.

When Balaam inquired concerning the Israelites, God said, "You shall not go with them; you shall not curse the people, for they are blessed." God was very clear and emphatic; do not go with Balak and do not curse Israel.

When King Balak heard the disappointing news, he sent again to Balaam the same request. But this time he offered him more money and honor. So Balaam asked God a second time. At this point in the story, one has to ponder which part of "no" did Balaam not understand? The only thing that had changed was the amount of money and prestige that King Balak was offering.

Which part of "no" did Balaam not understand? The only thing that had changed was the amount of money and prestige that King Balak was offering

Ironically, God allowed the prophet to go, but the Scriptures record, "God's anger was aroused because he went." The prophet was obviously interested in the money and as Balaam went, the Angel of the Lord stood in his way with his sword drawn. And God opened the mouth of Balaam's donkey to reason with the mad prophet about his covetous pursuit. His willingness to follow revealed a spirit of selfishness.

The story is hysterical because the mad prophet was so focused on the possible reward that he argues with a talking donkey. It illustrates the folly of covetousness. A covetous spirit will cause a man to lose his reasoning faculties. The talking donkey was God's way of showing the prophet his stupidity. If God said "no", did he really think God might change His mind if Balak offered more money?

The Apostle Peter uses the example of Balaam to illustrate the insanity of the end time generation. He says, "But these, like natural brute beasts made to be caught and destroyed, speak evil of the things they do not understand, And will utterly perish in their own

> *The talking donkey was God's way of showing the prophet his stupidity*

corruption...They have forsaken the right way and gone astray, following the way of Balaam...who loved the wages of unrighteousness; but was rebuked for his iniquity: a dumb donkey speaking with a man's voice restrained the madness of the prophet...While they promise them liberty, they themselves are slaves of corruption; for by whom a person is overcome, by him also he is brought into bondage."[7] To be caught up in the pursuit of the microchip identity is to follow in the way of Balaam.

The Money Changers

Did you know that Jesus can get very angry? Jesus threw the money changers out of the temple twice. The first time was at the beginning of His public ministry and the second time was three years later, just before He was crucified. The stories are told in John 2 and Matthew 21. Jesus constructed a whip of cords to physically motivate the merchants to leave. In His zeal, He flipped over their tables, scattering their coins and merchandise across the floor.

> *This scene of public disturbance is not the same picture of meek and mild Jesus holding a lamb on the Sunday School wall.*

This scene of public disturbance is not the same picture of meek and mild Jesus holding a lamb on the Sunday School wall. What could possibly have angered the Messiah to throw merchants out of His Father's house? After all, the people did need the oxen, sheep and doves for their sacrifices. The answer is simple; a covetous spirit will always get you thrown out of God's house.

"The money changers made a business of accommodating those who did not have the Jewish half-shekel for the annual temple tax."[8] They refused to accept foreign money with images of the Roman emperors under the false pretense of the second commandment, which forbade graven images. Thus, "A surcharge was made and the way opened for various malpractices."[9] The money changers profited from the highly lucrative sale of sacrificial animals. Plus, they made extra income off the forced exchange of Roman coins to the half-shekel.

Their pious keeping of the second commandment disguised their hypocrisy to violate the tenth commandment, "You shall not covet." The whole temple atmosphere was charged with profiteering. Jesus cried out, "Take these things away! Do not make My Father's house a house of merchandise!"[10] Three years later Jesus confirmed their unrepentant corruption when He grieved, "It is written, 'My house shall be called a house of prayer,' but you have made it a den of thieves.'"[11]

Covetousness is Alive and Well

The spirit of covetousness continues to destroy the church, nation and world today. The church turns off many people because of an over-emphasis on money. Instead of seeing people hungry for God, seeking His righteousness and praying for the salvation of the world, they see TV evangelists flashing gold watches and promising the saints prosperity if they will give more.

Like Elisha's day, it is not time for these things. It is time to return to the heart of God who desires to bring healing. We need to recognize the spirit of our day and cry out for an awakening to His lovingkindness and salvation.

The nation boasts, "In God We Trust." Our puritan forefathers came to "*New* England" to pursue freedom from the tyranny of old England and freedom of religion. Their pursuit of religious freedom gave birth to America as a "Christian Nation" as men pursued biblical principles in glorifying Jesus Christ.

But freedom has evolved. Today, freedom means freedom *from* religion and freedom to pursue opportunities for wealth with abandonment. I suspect this American god in whom men trust is an evolving deity, made in the likeness of man for man's own convenience. Like the temple money changers, their pious confessions seem to mask their true covetous motives. This unrestrained spirit of covetousness is destroying the nation's character.

The Terrorist's Perspective

Please do not perceive these comments as a defense of terrorism. Murder and violence is wrong, and those who engage in such under the name of Allah will suffer the same eternal judgment of hell as those who follow covetousness in the name of God. God is no respecter of persons. But for the sake of understanding the destructive nature of covetousness, let us look through the eyes of a Muslim extremist.

In my travels to Arab countries, I have asked numerous Muslims why they hate America. Why do they see Americans as infidels, the agents of Satan? Their response usually invokes a common theme. "American capitalists are destroying our culture", they chide. "We are sick and tired of seeing our people wearing western clothing, Levi jeans, and t-shirts with Mickey Mouse," they lament. "We despise seeing satellite dishes on our neighbors' roof tops, piping in the Playboy channel, its destroying their religious zeal," they groan.

Suddenly, the motivation seems clear as to why Muslim extremists would seek to destroy the twin towers of New York. Those towers represented the culmination of American ingenuity; they were towering symbols of the strength of America's economy and culture.

The Muslim extremists view the "Christian Nation" across the ocean and they do not see godly men, contrite before God in their pursuit of righteous ideals. Instead, they see covetous men masking carnal pursuits with a facade of piety: "In God We Trust." The Muslim are really viewing the golden calf crowd growing strong in numbers.

Mohammed held the Jews in contempt for their covetous behavior in the Quran. The Quran states, "Remember... Moses, and in his absence you took the calf (for worship) and you did a grievous wrong."[12] The Muslim extremist perceives the same golden calf spirit in America and beholds the capitalist with disdain. To him this is war, and the covetous spirit must be destroyed.

Billy Graham's Exhortation

The collapse of the twin towers cut deep into the conscience of America. The terrorist event caused America to search its soul. Churches were suddenly filled as hungry men and women sought understanding for confused, wounded and opened hearts. With continuous newscasts replaying the video images of the collapsing towers, the nation listened to the President's Day of Prayer and Remembrance at the National Cathedral.

The Pastor of America, Reverend Billy Graham challenged the country to remember its foundation. He did this by using the twin towers as an illustration of the spiritual choice before America. Here is the excerpt:

"We all watched in horror, as planes crashed into the steel and glass of the World Trade Center. Those majestic towers built on solid foundations were examples of the prosperity and creativity of America. When damaged, those buildings eventually plummeted to the ground, imploding in upon themselves.

Billy Graham used the twin towers as an illustration of the spiritual choice before America

Yet underneath the debris is a foundation that was not destroyed. There in lies the truth of that old hymn that Andrew Young quoted, 'how firm a foundation.' Yes our nation has been attacked, buildings destroyed, lives lost, but now we have a choice. Whether to implode and disintegrate emotionally and spiritually, as a people and a nation, or whether we choose to become stronger through all of the struggle to rebuild on a solid foundation. And I believe that we are in the process of starting to rebuild on that foundation. *That foundation is our trust in God.* That's what this service is all about. And in that faith we have the strength to endure something as difficult and horrendous as what we have experienced this week. This has been a terrible week, with many tears, but also a week of great faith. Churches all across the country have called prayer meetings... and in the words of that familiar hymn that Andrew Young quoted, its says, 'Fear not, I am with thee, O be not dismayed, for I am thy God and will give thee aid, I'll strengthen thee and help thee, and cause thee to stand upon my righteous omnipotent hand.' My prayer today is that we will feel the loving arms of God wrapped around us and will know in our hearts that He will never forsake us as we trust in Him...and this is going to be a day we will remember as a day of victory."

Summary

America's spiritual weakness is the love of economic opportunity and all that money will buy. There is nothing wrong with enjoying material comforts. It is the disproportioned balance between money and God that is drawing America into the ancient cult of the golden calf. Like Solomon, this double life is dividing the nation.

Like the money changers, Americans lean towards hypocrisy with their confession of God, while disguising their lust for more money. American ingenuity is developing the microchip identity, so we can hold onto our lifestyles, while remaining secure from terrorists. But will Americans see the end result is an implanted chip in the hand that God has forbidden? Or will Americans ignore God's two thousand year old warning, like Balaam who did not understand the meaning of "no."

The devil does not care whether he destroys with a demonic spirit of murder, violence or covetousness. He is simply delighted to rob souls with whatever spirit that works. At present, his sinister spirit of covetousness is backing the nation into the tin can of deception. As the microchip identity is implemented, Elisha's words echo with truth, it is not time to pursue money, clothing and material goods.

The Muslim sees America's flaw. The question is; do we see our flaw? Our national pastor, Billy Graham has encouraged the nation to respond by rebuilding on the foundation of God. The question is, will you?

Part III

What Remains is More Glorious!

*"Here is the patience of the saints;
here are those who keep the commandments
of God and the faith of Jesus."
Revelation 14:12*

Eleven

What Remains is More Glorious!

"The Lord said: I have pardoned, according to your word; but truly, as I live, all the earth shall be filled with the glory of the LORD." Numbers 14:20-21

The Apostle Paul wrote, "What remains is much more glorious."[1] This verse is talking about the glory of the Holy Spirit that is available to the believer who follows God's heart. This glory was originally given to Moses when he received the Ten Commandments, the *second* time. If you remember, the first time he received the tablets of stone, he dashed them to pieces at the sight of Israel worshipping the golden calf. What transpired between the broken commandments and receiving the second set accompanied with God's glory is a helpful lesson in the wilderness journey. It's all about God's glory.

God's judgment to Israel for worshipping the golden calf was simple. God said to Moses, "Go up to a land flowing with milk and honey; for I will not go up in your midst, lest I consume you on the way, for you are a stiff-necked people."[2] This passage conveys the idea that it is entirely possible to head toward the promised land, partying along the way. But the question is; can one get there without God's presence?

Moses' Intercession

The idea of going forward without God's presence was repugnant to Moses, who cried out to God, "If Your Presence does not go with us, do not bring us up from here. For how then will it be known that Your people and I have found grace in Your sight, except You go with us? So we shall be separate, Your people and I, from all the people who are upon the face of the earth."[3]   The Christian is unique, *only* because of God's mercy and presence. The Christian's desert experience is not meant to be a party, but rather a deep sense of God's grace sustaining him in faith and patience.

> *The Christian is unique, only because of God's mercy and presence.*

When the microchip identity becomes mandatory and Christians lose the ability to buy and sell, it will be the glory of God's presence that will sustain them during their wilderness journey.

God's Glory

Moses sought the Lord to forgive the golden calf crowd and allow His presence to go with them. When Moses asked God, "Please, show me Your Glory," God relented of His wrath and granted the request in the following ways.

First, God gave Moses a unique experience. The Lord said, "Here is a place by Me, and you shall stand on the rock. So shall it be, while My glory passes by, that I will put you in the cleft of the rock, and will cover you with

My hand while I pass by. Then I will take away My hand, and you shall see My back..."[4] and He added, "I will make all My goodness pass before you, and I will proclaim the name of the Lord before you. I will be gracious to whom I will be gracious, and I will have compassion on whom I will have compassion."[5]

Secondly, God invited Moses back to the mountain to receive the Ten Commandments a second time. This time the writing of the commandments was accompanied with this experience. "Now the Lord descended in the cloud and stood with him there, and proclaimed...The Lord, The Lord God, merciful and gracious, longsuffering, and abounding in goodness and truth, keeping mercy for thousands, forgiving iniquity and transgression and sin, by no means clearing the guilty...."[6]

And *finally*, Moses bowed before God to request His presence for the journey. To which God agreed saying, "Behold, I make a covenant. Before all your people I will do marvels such as have not been done in all the earth, nor in any nation; and all the people among whom you are shall see the work of the Lord. For it is an awesome thing that I will do...."[7]

God's glory was expressed in the safety of the rock's cleft, the out-pouring of mercy and the covenant of His presence.

Moses' Experience

For Moses, the golden calf episode brought him to a new level of experiencing God. At first he was angry, which caused him to break God's laws and not even deliver them to the Hebrew. But then, he interceded and touched the heart of God. When Moses softened his heart and prayed, God softened and relented of His wrath. It was Moses' intercessions that saved the people from God's destruction.[8]

Like Moses, godly men can get angry with the golden calf crowd and simply write them off as a lost cause. In the heat of disgust they can withhold their prayers and dismiss the rebels for destruction. But this kind of attitude falls short of God's glory.

The glory of God came upon Moses, because Moses demonstrated God's own character. By his prayers, Moses showed grace and in return received grace for the people. His intercession showed forgiveness and in return received forgiveness for the nation. He spiritually reaped what he sowed.

As a result, the glory of God came upon Moses as he received the second set of commandments. The glory on Moses' face brilliantly displayed the presence of God who showed mercy and pledged to lead on through the wilderness journey, and promised to do marvels, wonders and an awesome thing with the people.

Moses experienced the glory for himself when God's hand covered him in the cleft of the rock. He experienced the glory of His grace and presence. And Moses experienced the glory when God sustained him for forty days and nights without food or water.[9]

What was the awesome thing God would do for His people? He was going to perform the physically impossible. God was going to take an entire nation of people across the desert wilderness and sustain them with food, clothing and water.

The Complaint

As the nation trudged toward the promised land, the people grew tired of the manna God provided every morning. Their complaining displeased the Lord. The Scriptures record, "Now the mixed multitude who were among them yielded to intense craving; so the children of Israel also wept again and said: 'Who will give us meat to eat? We remember the fish which we ate freely in Egypt, the cucumbers, the melons, leeks, the onions, and the garlic; but now our whole being is dried up; there is nothing at all except this manna before our eyes!'"[10]

The mixed multitude was the golden calf crowd, who was half hearted concerning the Lord. They soon forgot the misery of their former bondage in Egypt and only remembered the good things. In their covetousness, they asked, "Who will give us meat to eat?" In these last days, the golden calf crowd will certainly pose the same question to the Lord when the microchip identity becomes mandatory.

The question was not; "Can or will God provide?" because God was already providing the miracle manna, and they certainly had sheep and cattle for meat. The mixed multitude said they regretted leaving Egypt. So the question was more about their lust for delicacies than sustenance. God granted their wish, but was very angry with them.

The Rebellion

Unfortunately, when they got to the promise land, the people refused to go in because of the giants. The Hebrew complained, "We are not able to go up against this people, for they are stronger than we...all the people whom we saw in it are men of great stature...and we were like grasshoppers in our own sight, and so we were in their sight...Why has the Lord brought us to this land to fall...that our wives and children should become victims? Would it not be better for us to return to Egypt? So they said to one another, 'Let us select a leader and return to Egypt.'"[11]

In the duplicity of their hearts, the golden calf crowd once again yielded to their cravings, coupled with fear. Despite God's signs and wonders, they refused to believe God could overcome the giants. Instead they proposed choosing a leader, who would take them back to the ways of the world (Egypt).

In disgust, God decided to punish the Hebrew and disinherit them. Again Moses, ever the intercessor reasoned with God. "Now if you kill these people as one man, then the nations which have heard of Your fame will speak, saying, because the Lord was not able to bring this people to the land which He swore to give them, therefore He killed them in the wilderness."[12]

The issued had focused on God's name and glory once again. Could God successfully bring a nation across the desert to the promised land? Moses appealed to God's glory and implored, "Let the power of my Lord be great, just as You have spoken saying, the Lord is longsuffering and abundant in mercy, forgiving iniquity and transgression; but He by no means clears the guilty...Pardon the iniquity of this people, I pray, according to the greatness of Your mercy, just as You have forgiven this people, from Egypt until now."[13]

The Compromise

God relented and said, "I have pardoned, according to your word; but truly, as I live, all the earth shall be filled with the glory of the Lord."[14] The pardon allowed the nation to wander in the desert for forty years, proving God was able to sustain and bring them to the promise land. When the golden calf crowd heard the judgment, they immediately decided to go up to the promised land. But, without the presence of God, they were no match for the enemy who quickly defeated them. Eventually, they all perished of old age, having never known the thrill of defeating giants. Thus God answer the question, can you get to the promised land, partying along the way, without the presence of God? The answer is no!

God did a new thing to vindicate His name. He raised up a new generation that followed God's heart. They were the children of whom the golden calf crowd said would be victims, instead they conquered the promised land after forty years of wandering in the wilderness. Thus God glorified His name.

What Remains is More Glorious!

Today, a new wilderness journey is arising, that will ask the same questions of God. When the microchip identity is made mandatory and the new golden calf crowd has chosen their world

> *"But truly, as I live, all the earth shall be filled with the glory of the Lord"*

leader, they will be pondering; can God deliver Christians during this desert season, when they cannot buy or sell because they have refused the implanted microchip? Can God provide sustenance in this economic wilderness and deliver them to the promise land? Can these Christians overcome the giant rulers of the land who are against them, having no way to purchase goods?

Remember God said, "But truly, as I live, all the earth shall be filled with the glory of the Lord."[15] God has every intention of showing the world His glory in these last days. He plans to fill the earth with the knowledge of

His power and glory. What better way than to have the world chiding His saints that they will not be able to survive unless they "get chipped". Yet God's glory will show His saints mercy, hiding them in the cleft of the rock, and covenanting to go with them in the journey just like Moses.

Remember, the Apostle Paul wrote, "Now all these things happened to them as examples, and they were written for our admonition, upon whom the ends of the ages have come."[16] The golden calf story is purposely recorded for discerning Christians to understand the last days. It is really the golden calf crowd that perishes in the wilderness, holding onto their worldly leader, having never understood God's glory and grace, and never overcoming the giants.

Yes, "What remains is much more glorious."[17] Why? Because there is a new generation in these last days, which holds to the commandments of God, not written on cold stones that crumble at the sight of the golden calf. These commands are written in their hearts, drawing on the glory of God. The countenance of these saints shines brightly the presence of God.

The prophet Haggai proclaimed, "According to the word I covenanted with you when you came out of Egypt, so My Spirit remains among you; do not fear!…Once more (it is a little while) I will shake the heavens and earth, the sea and dry land; and I will shake all nations, and they shall come to the Desire of All Nations, and I will fill this temple [the saints] with glory…The silver is Mine, and the gold is Mine,…The glory of this latter temple shall be greater than the former, …And in this place I will give peace says the Lord of host.."[18] Christians, get ready! For, "What remains is much more glorious!"

Twelve

Dominion Like Jesus

"He raised Him from the dead and seated Him at His right hand in the heavenly places, far above all principality and power and might and dominion, and every name that is named, not only in this age but also in that which is to come. And He put all things under His feet, and gave Him to be head over all things to the church." Ephesians 1:20-22

The ancient cult of the golden calf has re-emerged in the microchip identity as men begin to embrace the world's answer for terrorism that offers peace, safety, and sustenance. How should Christians prepare themselves for this season, when they refuse the chip and are no longer able to buy and sell? No doubt, as these events evolve God will raise up godly men like, "The sons of Issachar who had understanding of the times, to know what Israel ought to do."[1] But the answers are simple. There is no need to cower in fear, stockpiling food or hiding in remote places. We simply need God's heart.

The secular world is dealing with the fear of terrorism and the desire to hang onto their current way of life. Their answer is to give everyone a positive identity so authorities can track the movement of money and people to enhance safety. Thus, men can continue to buy, sell, and prosper without hindrance. But Christians already have these blessings provided for us by God. We have our identity in Christ, and God is our source and protector.

Prosperity is defined by its goals. If one's ambitions is to have a large estate before death, then ignoring God and receiving the microchip identity is logical. But if one's ambition is to honor God and live for eternity, then receiving the mark is lunacy. Especially in light of God's warning of the loss of salvation to all who receive the mark.

Having Dominion Like Jesus

When God created mankind, He said, "Let Us make man in Our image, according to Our likeness; let them have dominion...over all the earth."[2] That dominion is to be in the likeness of God and His Son Jesus. Several events in the life of Jesus are examples of having dominion over the earth.

When Jesus fed the multitudes with five loaves and two small fish, the people were astonished. Anyone who could produce food and feed multitudes ought to be made king they thought. "Therefore when Jesus perceived that they were about to come and take Him by force to make Him king, He departed again to the mountain by Himself alone."[3]

Jesus did not come to be *a* king, for being *a* king was not necessarily having "dominion over the earth." God's plan was much greater; Jesus was destined to be "King of Kings." Hence, prosperity is better defined as doing the will of God, than being just *a* king.

Another event that defines "having dominion over the earth" is Satan's temptation of Jesus in the wilderness. The devil showed Jesus, "All the kingdoms of the world in a moment of time. And the devil said to Him, 'All this authority I will give You, and their glory; for this has been delivered to me,

> *Jesus did not come to be a king, for being a king was not necessarily having "dominion over the earth"*

and I give it to whomever I wish. Therefore, if You will worship before me, all will be yours.'" Of course Jesus refused and declared, "Get behind me Satan! For it is written, 'You shall worship the Lord your God, and Him only you shall serve.'"[4] Again, God's plan for Jesus was much greater. Jesus could have been lord of the earth had He bowed to Satan, but God's plan was to be "Lord of Lords" and sit at the right hand of the Father in heaven.

The same temptation is being offered in the microchip identity. An individual can receive the authority to pursue wealth within all the kingdoms of the world. But to do so is to submit to the puppet of Satan, the Anti-Christ, as one's source of sustenance. True spiritual dominion puts these earthly desires behind and submits only to the Lordship of Christ. This is dominion in the likeness of Jesus.

Kingdom Truth

The best demonstration of having dominion over the world is the cross of Jesus. When Pilate questioned Jesus about being the King of the Jews, Jesus answered, "My kingdom is not of this world. If My kingdom were of this world, My servants would fight." Pilate then asked, "Are You a king then?" Jesus answered, "You say rightly that I am a king. For this cause I was born, and for this cause I have come into the world, that I should bear witness to the truth...Pilate said to Him, 'What is truth?' And when he had said this, he went out again to the Jews, and said to them, 'I find no fault in Him at all.'"[5]

The truth is; Jesus came to be King of Kings and to demonstrate His divine nobility by going to the cross. He could have called upon ten thousand angels to deliver Him, but chose not too. Though Jesus was perfectly innocent, He died for the sins of the world, fulfilling God's will, "For God so loved the world that He gave His only begotten Son, that whoever believes in Him should not perish but have everlasting life."[6] Thus God exalted Jesus to the right hand of power, as King of Kings.

When the microchip identity becomes mandatory, genuine Christians will follow Christ's example when they refuse to receive the mark. The Scriptures forewarn of the Anti-Christ, "It was granted to him to make war with the saints and to overcome them. And authority was given him over every tribe, tongue, and nation."[7] Just as Caesar persecuted Jesus, so the Anti-Christ will persecute Christians.

But this season of persecution reveals the kingdom of God as told in this scripture; "I heard a loud voice in heaven, 'Now is salvation, and strength, and the kingdom of our God, and the power of His Christ have come, for the accuser [Satan] of our brethren, who accused them before our God day and night, has been cast down. And they overcame him by the blood of the Lamb and by the word of their testimony, and they did not love their lives to the death.'"[8] This is true kingdom living, the willingness to follow Christ by dying to the world in obedience to God. This is dominion over the world in the likeness of Jesus.

Paul's Example

Jesus said of Satan, "The thief does not come except to steal, and to kill, and to destroy."[9] This thievery is certainly true of Satan's end time plan concerning the identity chip. Consider this verse, "Every man should eat and drink and enjoy the good of all his labor, it is the gift of God."[10] But Satan seeks to steal this gift away by prohibiting anyone from buying or selling who does not have the microchip identity.

When the microchip identity becomes mandatory, Christians will need to scale back their standard of living. They will enter a season of living modestly, just as the Apostle Paul did. In the process of fulfilling God's will, Paul said, "I have learned in whatever state I am, to be content: I know how to

> *"Every man should eat and drink and enjoy the good of all his labor, it is the gift of God." But Satan seeks to destroy this gift by implementing the microchip identity*

be abased, and I know how to abound. Everywhere and in all things I have learned both to be full and to be hungry, both to abound and to suffer need. I can do all things through Christ who strengthens me."[11] Learning to live modestly is wisdom. It prepares the heart to be content in God, not in worldly possessions.

Food, drink, and the fruit of our labors are indeed the gift of God. But listen to what Paul said in regards to these things when it comes to following Christ. He said, "All things are lawful for me, but all things are not helpful. All things are lawful for me, but I will not be brought under the power of any. Foods for the stomach and the stomach for foods, but God will destroy both it and them."[12] Paul is simply saying, if I have to make a choice, I will choose Christ rather than tarnish my testimony before men.

Paul further emphasized, "Do not destroy the work of God for the sake of food. All things are indeed pure, but it is evil for the man who eats with offense."[13] Genuine Christians understand that if faced with the decision to take the microchip identity so they can continue their current lifestyle, they will choose a life of faith instead.

Paul pleaded with God concerning the trials of following Christ. And God replied, "My grace is sufficient for you, for My strength is made perfect in weakness. 'Therefore most gladly I will rather boast in my infirmities, that the power of Christ may rest upon me. Therefore I take pleasure in infirmities, in reproaches, in needs, in persecutions, in distresses, for Christ's sake. For when I am weak, then I am strong.'"[14]

There is a dimension of faith that only a few Christians have ever come to know. American Christians have lived in a prosperous nation with a high standard of living. But somewhere in the life of faith, there is a place of knowing God's strength and power in the midst of difficult times. That life of faith brings contentment, peace, power, gladness, and boasting in God, even in harsh circumstances. It is this kind of faith that will enable Christians to have dominion over the earth during the mandated microchip identity.

Kingdom Confusion

The gospel writer says of the disciples, "They thought the kingdom of God would appear immediately."[15] Their anticipation of the Messiah was the restoration of Israel to its glory days under King David and King Solomon. This explains why they wanted to make Jesus a king.

When Jesus began to show the disciples that He must go to Jerusalem and suffer many things, be crucified and raised the third day, Peter took Jesus aside and rebuked the Lord saying, "Far be it from You, Lord; this shall not happen to You!" But note what the Lord said to Peter, "Get behind Me Satan! You are an offense to Me, for you are not mindful of the things of God, but the things of men."[16] The disciples were not thinking about suffering, they were thinking like worldly-minded people, about ruling in the new government with power.

Their thinking was faulty. While the disciples were arguing over who would be the greatest in the new government, James and John were getting their mother to ask Jesus if they could sit on His right of power. When Jesus reiterated, "Let these words sink down into your ears, for the Son of Man is about to be betrayed into the hands of men", the Bible records, "But they did not understand this saying, and it was hidden from them so that they did not perceive it; and they were afraid...."[17] They were focused on the things of men, not on the things of God. This worldly focus produced fear and confusion.

When the disciples were coveting worldly positions of greatness, Jesus asked a simple question. He said, "Are you able to drink from the cup that I am about to drink, and be baptized with the baptism that I am baptized with?"[18] Jesus is asking the same question today. Baptism is the willingness to go to the cross if need be, to lay down one's life in obedience to God and refuse to "get chipped" even if it means not being able to buy or sell.

Are You Able?

Today it is the same. I find very few are willing to consider the possibility that Christians may have to suffer in these last days. They seem fearful of even discussing the microchip identity. The idea of cutting back their lifestyle is dreadful. Their hearts seem to be mired down in golden calf worship. But this is faulty thinking. This kind of thinking does not understand the power of Christ to have dominion over the world.

After His crucifixion and resurrection, Jesus hid His countenance as He walked with two of His disciples on the road to Emmaus. They were sad, as they discussed Jesus' crucifixion. Jesus said to them, "O foolish ones, and slow of heart to believe in all that the prophets have spoken! Ought not the Christ to have suffered these things and to enter into His glory?"[19] Take note; there was glory in overcoming the world. The suffering was God's plan, and that plan was for exaltation of His Son.

It is God's plan in these last days to bring a test upon the whole world with the identity chip. Genuine Christians may plead with God concerning the trials, but like Paul, they will learn to take pleasure in their weaknesses, knowing that it reveals the grace and strength of the Lord.

Remember what Paul said, "That I may know Him and the power of His resurrection, and the fellowship of His sufferings, being conformed to His death, if by any means, I may attain the resurrection from the dead. Not that I have already attained, or am already perfected; but I press on, that I may lay hold of that for which Christ Jesus has also laid hold of me...forgetting those things which are behind and reaching forward to those things which are ahead, I press toward the goal for the prize of the upward call of God in Christ Jesus. Therefore let us, as many as are mature, have this mind...."[20]

God created us to live in this day and hour, in these last days. We have a great calling. Jesus laid hold of us for a reason and that reason is to demonstrate obedience in the midst of a disobedient world. There is a goal, a prize. To be identified with the divine nature of God, having dominion over the world. We have faith to believe, or God would not have chosen us for this hour.

Consider this passage, "Let us run with endurance the race that is set before us, looking unto Jesus, the author and finisher of our faith, who for the joy that was set before Him endured the cross."[21] Jesus endured the cross for the joy that was to come as a result of His obedience. Likewise, we must recognize there is a cross to be endured and a joy to come as we set our focus on Christ.

James in his epistle said, "My brethren, take the prophets, who spoke in the name of the Lord, as an example of suffering and patience. Indeed we count them blessed who endure. You have heard of the perseverance of Job and seen the end intended by the Lord that the Lord is very compassionate and merciful."[22]

Yes, Job was tested because Satan claimed he only loved God for his many possessions. God's plan was to use Job's obedience as a witness to the heavenly beings of a pure faith. Afterwards, God rewarded Job immensely. It is the same for the end time Christian.

Extremists

There are many who are fighting for a kingdom. Muslim extremists enforce their will upon the masses with terror. And ultra right-wing Christians bomb abortion clinics, while militia groups in America plot strategies against the government. There will always be another Osama Bin Laden or Timothy McVeigh waiting in the shadows. It is because of terrorism, that national identification has been expedited to the forefront of America's conscience.

The microchip identity is the social architect's defense so present governments can hold onto their kingdoms. Extremists survive in anonymity. The extremists will not receive the identity chip lest they be exposed. Unfortunately, Christians who are praying for their governments and all who are in power so we can lead peaceful lives will be labeled with the extremists, because we will not receive the microchip identity either. Christians will be viewed as unpatriotic, disloyal, and traitors.

Summary

It is easy to see how Christians, who have done nothing wrong, will be persecuted. Pilate said of Jesus, "I find no fault in Him." Like Jesus, Christians will suffer the wrongs of others in fulfilling God's will. But in doing so, we demonstrate belief in a kingdom that is not of this world. Like Jesus, we will love our fellow man, even though they miss-label us as terrorists and a danger to society. We will pray for their salvation and the opening of their eyes to the prophecy concerning the microchip identity. We will scale back our lifestyles and seek debt free living in preparation for this social evolution. We will bring our lives into balance as we return to God-centered living. As a result, our divided nation will witness a great revival as many turn to the Lord, while the golden calf crowd is caught up in the great falling away. And Christians will have dominion over the world because "what remains is more glorious."

Thirteen

What Should Christians Do?

*"A prudent man foresees evil and hides himself,
but the simple pass on and are punished." Proverbs 22:3*

Did you ever ride a seesaw as a kid? The thrill of
bouncing up and down could be lots of fun. However, if
the local bully who was bigger than you jumped on the
other end, the fun evaporated. Suddenly you found
yourself jacked up into the air, trapped by his
overwhelming weight, and pondering how to get off. The
seesaw was fun when two people of equal weight got on
it, but miserable when out of balance.

The Covetous Bully

It was only a few decades ago that most Americans
echoed a familiar sentiment about life. They would speak
of life's priorities as, "God, family and country." Today
the golden calf crowd is saying, "It's all about me." Their
priorities are out of balance and many who are caught up
in the "me generation" are finding themselves trapped. In
an effort to have it all, they have been ensnared by

massive debt for homes, furniture, automobiles, and credit cards.

As a result, they work twenty-four-seven and have little time for God. Meanwhile, their family life breaks down from the stress of debt and work. Like an overweight bully on the other end of the seesaw, covetousness is grounding America's spiritual character. This generation is proving the wisdom of an old saying, "Money is a good servant, but a poor master."

> *"Money is a good servant, but a poor master"*

Our divided nation has many who love God, but in the confusion of priorities they are caught up in covetousness and are slowly losing their first love. Those who do not profess God are simply pursuing selfish ambition and the growing masses of these two groups are the overweight bully. God's people need to repent and help bring our nation back into balance. Revival begins with the house of God. Therefore, we should strive for the healing of our nation by returning to god-centered priorities. This is what Christians should do.

Christian Responsibility

The Christian's ambition in life should be first and foremost, to honor God. Our identity should be to conform to His image. As the microchip identity unfolds, the vanity of golden calf worship becomes clearer in light of the words of Jesus, "For whoever desires to save his life will lose it, but whoever loses his life for My sake and the gospel's will save it."[1] Eventually the Christian will not be allowed to buy or sell for refusing to take the identity chip. So it is wisdom to live modestly with contentment. Learning to do without now will soften the trauma of not being able to buy or sell when the microchip identity becomes mandatory.

Jesus promised His disciples the "abundance of life." Consider this passage, "His divine power has given to us all things that pertain to life and godliness, through the knowledge of Him who called us by glory and virtue, by which have been given to us exceeding great and precious

> *"His divine power has given to us all things that pertain to life and godliness"*

promises, that through these you may be partakers of the divine nature, having escaped the corruption that is in the world though lust."[2] Wow, what a promise! If we will grow in the knowledge of God, walking in obedience, we will partake of His divine nature and receive *all things* that pertain to life and godliness. Life lived to its fullest is a life walking in Christ.

The corruption of the world has blinded men to what life is all about. The meaning of life is unclear. When questions of law are challenged in court, it is the responsibility of the Supreme Court to decide what those laws mean. The court makes their decisions base on the original intent of the founding fathers in the constitution. Likewise, let us rediscover the original intent of God when He created man. The foundational principles of creation are found in the first pages of the Bible.

Creation's Principles

When God created man in His own image, only a few dynamics were taking place in the Garden of Eden. First, man observed God resting on the seventh day of creation and enjoyed fellowship with Him. Secondly, man and woman were created in the image of God. They were an expression of His nature and loved one another. And third, man was given the task of dressing the garden.

When you think about it, those three aspects are the essence of life today. There are three great decisions you will make in a lifetime. First, will you follow God? Second, who will you marry and third, what kind of work will you do in serving your community? Those decisions and how you approach each one can bring a multitude of blessings, or a multitude of curses.

Plus, if you get them out of balance with each other, life becomes a mess. The man who focuses on work alone becomes a workaholic. The person who is preoccupied with sex becomes a fornicator, adulterer, or pervert. And we have all heard of the individual who is "so heavenly minded that he is of no earthly good."

> *Three creation principles bring fullness to mankind: Resting in God, Enjoying Family, and Work*

God intended for these three principles to bring fullness to mankind; resting in God, enjoying family, and work. When individuals choose to be celibate, then the focus should be on serving God and mankind, as was the case with such noted individuals as Jesus, Apostle Paul and Mother Teresa. Let us review these simple principles.

Principle One: The Seventh Day of Creation

"Remember the Sabbath day to keep it holy", is the fourth of the Ten Commandments. Originally, God did not command Adam and Eve to obey this commandment. Instead, the Scriptures say, "And on the seventh day God ended His work which He had done, and He rested on the seventh day from all His work which He had done. Then God blessed the seventh day and sanctified it, because in it He rested from all His work which God had created and made."[3] There is no command to follow, no rule or law, just the example of God. God does not want mankind under laws of do's and don'ts. He wants us to follow His Spirit.

When God breathed life into Adam, he must have suddenly awakened and looked around in awe and wonder of creation. He must have pondered what the mystery of life was all about and decided the one who knew was the one hovering over him. As he walked and talked with God, he experienced several things about the seventh day of creation.

First, Adam experienced worship. The euphoria of being alive overflowed in celebrating the Creator. Secondly, he enjoyed the presence or company of God. Third, he came to understand what it means to be sanctified or set apart for God's service. And finally, Adam rested. All of these facets should be true of attending church today.

Adam's brand new body hardly needed rest. He had a whole new world to explore. Plus, Eve certainly needed companionship, and the garden was there to prune. But, Adam spent the first full day of his life walking and resting with God.

> *Resting in God is discovering the Author of life has provided everything*

Resting in God is discovering the Author of life has provided everything. There is no need to be anxious, to worry or fret over the future. God had even provided salvation for Adam and Eve, even though they had not yet sinned. The Scriptures declare, "The Lamb slain from the foundation of the world."[4] God in His magnificent love for mankind had taken care of his every need. No amount of work on Adam's part could possibly make God love him anymore than God already did.

Today it is the same. God longs for creation to rest in Him. The Scriptures say, "If God be for us, who can be against us? He who spared not His own Son, but delivered Him up for us all, how shall He not with Him also freely give us all things?"[5]

Christians need to return to the house of the Lord, one day in every seven, to rest in God. In church we will learn to worship God for life itself and experience His presence. There we will discover that God has a purpose for creating us in this day and hour. By resting in God, He will provide for our every need.

Covetousness perverts the seventh day of creation. Instead of pursuing God, men pursue selfish ambitions. Their lust yearns for materialism. That carnal spirit is developing a microchip to access the goods of the world, in spite of God's warnings against the humanistic solution. Instead of loving and serving God, men love and serve themselves.

What shall we do in light of the microchip identity? Let us return to worship. The seventh day is blessed. This means experiencing God's rest is an ongoing dynamic of creation. The Author of life is still imparting life and He will see us through the microchip identity season ahead. When Christians trust God, personal revival comes and results in restoring the moral conscience of America.

Principle Two: Family

The Scripture says, "In the day that God created man, He made him in the likeness of God. He created them male and female, and blessed them and called them Mankind in the day they were created."[6] God's image is reflected in both the man and the woman. One cannot really understand God without understanding the nature of the opposite sex.

Man's desire for woman and woman's desire for man is not just physical, but a spiritual yearning for the completeness the one gives to the other. Thus, man is a guardian to the woman and woman is a helpmate to the man.

> *God's image is reflected in both, the man and the woman*

God's nature is all-powerful and full of judgment as seen in the Old Testament laws. Hence, a man tends to be strong and rational as he reflects God's image in physical strength and logic. On the other hand, God is seen as patient, forgiving, merciful and kind in the New Testament, extending grace and forgiveness for sins through Jesus Christ. Hence, a woman tends to be emotional, showing kindness and gentleness as she reflect God's image in femininity and passion.

The sexual union is not just physical, but a culmination of devotion of one to the other in appreciation of their unique expression of God. This completeness is the atmosphere God desires for raising children, in order that they may grow in the knowledge of truth and mercy. Consider the Psalmist's poetic affirmation of the glory of God, "Mercy and truth have met together; Righteousness and peace have kissed."[7] God's nature is uniquely expressed in both man and woman, in strength and grace, in logic and emotion.

Covetousness perverts God's marriage foundation, reducing relationships to the physical. Today, people just live together as they pursue education and careers. Thus, placing a higher priority on their careers. Their careers do not serve the relationship; the relationship is subservient to their careers.

If the couple does marry, often the pursuit of materialism and success requires such enormous energy and commitment that it strains the bonds of marriage. Since the relationship was not built with God as the highest priority, the union tears under the pressure of bill collectors. Satan's plan is to destroy the family so he can destroy the children by giving them an unbalanced perspective of God.

As society wanders further and further from God's foundational principle for marriage, man waxes worse and worse in perversion. Today, the world views male and female relationships in the context of the physical. Marketing advertisements fill billboards, TV screens and magazines with images of sensuality. Movies and television rarely depict man and woman in wholesome marriage relationships. Instead, they are seen as socially acceptable cohabiters.

The feminist crowd feels no need for the man, as many seek to have children through surgical conception. And men chuckle to one another, "Why buy the cow when you can get the milk free?" Ultimately, the woman rejects the man and turns to the woman for physical fulfillment and men do the same, resulting in lesbianism and homosexuality. The world seeks to use and abuse one another because of their self-centered ambitions. "It's all about me", they reason.

Sensuality is rampant, yet men and women are still not satisfied. It is time to return to God's foundations. Marriage is part of God's plan to give mankind, "all things that pertain to life and Godliness." When a man and woman enter marriage reverently, adoring each other's unique expression of God, fullness and completeness result. This feeling of wholeness diminishes one's need for materialism.

By shedding ourselves of covetousness and focusing on God, we see the world differently. Instead of needing the best of everything, from clothes to furniture and cars to homes, we learn to make do with only that which is necessary. This will require less expense and strain on income, freeing up more time for commitment to relationships and God. No one ever said on his deathbed, "I wish I had bought a Porsch", instead he says, "I wish I had spent more time with my wife, my children and knowing God." These are the important values in life. Christians need to restore the foundational principle of family.

Principle Three: Work

God gave man the responsibility of work for personal fulfillment. Work was not a punishment for sin because God gave the job of dressing the garden before the fall. Genesis records, "The Lord God took the man and put him in the Garden of Eden to tend it and keep it... saying, 'Of every tree of the garden you may eat freely' [except the tree of the knowledge of good and evil]."[8]

Apparently God visited Adam "in the cool of the day" for fellowship and perhaps to look at the garden. Through the garden man was given the opportunity to have dominion over the earth. The garden yielded fruit for Adam and Eve and met their physical needs. And the garden gave man a sense of being responsible to God who created it. No doubt, Adam must have shared with God the fruits of the garden, as they walked together.

Satan uses the spirit of covetousness to pervert God's plan for work in many ways. Many employees see work as a curse and seek to get away with as much as they can through laziness. In contrast, employers try to work their salaried employees overtime (more than is reasonable) in an effort to get more for less. Each distrusts the other and seeks to take advantage of one another.

Covetousness is seen in businesses that abandon the principle of service. They use deception and dishonesty to increase profits. The spirit of the company becomes one of serving the greed of its corporate executives instead of serving the public and providing for its employees.

Individuals manifest selfishness when they seek to keep the fruit of their labors to themselves, instead of sharing with God, as did Adam. As a result the covetous spirit deepens its roots and as economic opportunity increases, the individual seeks to make more and more money to buy more and more things to the exclusion of God.

The Apostle John takes note of this spirit. "Do not love the world or the things in the world. If anyone loves the world, the love of the Father is not in him. For all that is in the world, the lust of the flesh, the lust of the eyes, and the pride of life, is not of the Father but is of the world. And the world is passing away, and the lust of it; but he who does the will of God abides forever."[9]

> *"He who loves silver will not be satisfied with silver; nor he who loves abundance with increase."*

The carnal man seeks wealth with selfish motives. Wealth apart from God has an appearance of preeminence. This is called pride. But getting one's dwelling pictured in a "Home and Garden" magazine will never substitute for the Lamb's Book of Life. Nor will affluence alone bring fulfillment. The Scriptures declare, "He who loves silver will not be satisfied with silver; Nor he who loves abundance, with increase."[10]

In fact, greed can make one extremely wealthy, yet pitifully poor. Consider Jesus' words in light of the microchip identity. "Because you say, 'I am rich, have become wealthy and have need of nothing' and do not know that you are wretched, miserable, poor, blind, and naked, "I counsel you to buy from Me gold refined in the fire, that you may be rich; and white garments, that you may be clothed, that the shame of your nakedness may not be revealed; and anoint your eyes with eye salve, that you may see."[11]

Without spiritual insight, a covetous person will receive the microchip identity to the loss of their salvation. He may be rich in the world, but he is poor in faith. This is to his shame and

> *Greed can make one extremely wealthy, yet pitifully poor*

nakedness, that he did not understand life in light of eternity.

The proper way to view work is to understand a job as a stewardship from the Lord. That stewardship is an opportunity to serve God and one's fellowman. And in return enjoy the fruits of one's labor. The Apostle Paul speaks of a promise when having a godly attitude about work. He says we are to work, "Not with eyeservice, as menpleasers, but as bond servants of Christ, doing the will of God from the heart, with goodwill doing service, as to the Lord, and not to men, knowing that whatever good anyone does, he will receive the same from the Lord...."[12] This kind of attitude is of great value to any employer.

Once the microchip identity becomes mandatory, Christians will not be able to receive an income like they do today. But if they have excellent skills and work ethics, they will still be able to work. Employers will construct unique working relationships to accommodate those who refuse the implanted microchip. However, if one's attitude is selfish or lazy, it will be extremely difficult to get an employer to keep you working.

The Hispanics in America are proof of this truth. Many are illegal. So how do they work and maintain sustenance? Many employers have houses rented where the Hispanics live. The boss provides transportation back and forth to work and groceries to the house. Why? The Hispanics are excellent workers who appreciate the opportunity. They treat the employer with respect and because they come from a land where people have very little, they rejoice in what little they are given.

When the identity chip becomes mandatory, employers will do the same for Christians if their work ethics are good. Christians will be able to survive not being able to buy or sell, just like many Hispanics today. The movie, "Schindlers' List" is a testimony of this very principle, depicting the survival of many Jews who worked for sustenance, not money during the Holocaust. Our well-being is enhanced when we learn to work "unto the Lord", and not with selfish motives.

Prayer and Intercession

The prophet said, "My people are destroyed for lack of knowledge."[13] There are multitudes of people who are the "blind following the blind" as they worship the golden calf. Christian hearts should be as God's heart. God loves mankind and longs for them to be saved. When given opportunity to speak with individuals about the prophetic utterances of God, we should tell them of God's love and warnings, and we should pray.

> *There are multitudes of people who are the "blind following the blind" as they worship the golden calf*

Moses was spoken of as a friend of God. When Moses discovered the Israelites had made the golden calf, he initially responded with anger. Then, true to his priestly role, he prayed. The Psalmist says, "Therefore He [God] said that He would destroy them, Had not Moses His chosen one stood before Him in the breach, to turn away His wrath, lest He destroy them."[14] Yes, God would have destroyed them had it not been for the intercession of Moses. Prayer and leadership led the nation to repentance.

> *God would have destroyed them had it not been for the intercession of Moses. Prayer and leadership led the nation to repentance.*

The Prophet Nehemiah writes, "Even when they made a molded calf for themselves, and said, 'This is your god'...Yet in Your manifold mercies You did not forsake them in the wilderness. The pillar of the cloud did not depart from them by day, to lead them on the road; nor the pillar of fire by night, to show them light, and the way they should go. You also gave them Your good Spirit to instruct them, and did not withhold Your manna from their mouth, and gave them water for their thirst. Forty years You sustained them in the wilderness; They lacked nothing; Their clothes did not wear out and their feet did not swell."[15] The historical forty-year journey through the wilderness is proof that God is able to provide for all who repent of golden calf worship.

Summary

What should Christians do? Christians need to pray for God's mercy for the golden calf crowd. Ask God to open their eyes and see the condition of the earth and their souls, so they will repent. Perhaps God will grant revival and turn the prophetic clock back, allowing Christians to live in peace.

Our responsibility is to conform to the image of God. By following God's original creation principles, we can restore godly balance. That example will give our divided nation a pattern to follow. Hopefully, we can restore our nation's Christian values to the point of bringing the covetous bully back into balance. But should the golden calf worshippers prevail with their microchip identity, God will provide.

Fourteen

Our Joseph-Jesus Provider!

*"You meant evil against me; but God meant it for good,
in order to bring it about as it is this day, to save many
people alive...Do not be afraid; I will provide for you and
your little ones." –Joseph   Genesis 50:20-21*

The story of Joseph is told in the Old Testament
chapters of Genesis 37-50. Once again, let's be reminded
that the Apostle Paul said of Old Testament stories, "Now
all these things happened to them as examples, and they
were written for our admonition, upon whom the ends of
the ages have come."[1] There are many parallels between
Joseph and Jesus and ironically between Joseph and the
Anti-Christ. These parallels give insight and reveal the
faithfulness of God to provide for His people.

Here is the story of Joseph. Joseph was the favorite
son of Jacob who gave him a coat of many colors and the
responsibility of checking on his brothers. His brothers
sold Joseph into slavery for giving their father a bad
report. Once in Egypt God raised up Joseph, by allowing
him to interpret a dream about cows and to sit at the right
hand of Pharaoh. Although his brothers meant to do
Joseph harm, God's plan was to provide for Jacob's

family during the coming famine. Joseph became the focal point of providing bread to all nations.

Joseph: A Shadow of Jesus

There are many parallels between Joseph and Jesus. Through these similarities, we can understand that God was communicating His plans for the redemption of Israel. The Hebrew name Joseph means, "May God add other sons." Likewise, Jesus' name means "Savior" and conveys the idea of adding others to the kingdom of God.

> *Joseph's exalted name, "Zaphenath-paneah" means, "God speaks-He lives!"*

When Pharaoh exalted Joseph to the right hand of power, he changed Joseph's name to "Zaphenath-paneah" which means, "God speaks-He lives!" In like manner, it is written of Jesus, "God...has in these last days spoken to us by His Son...who being in the brightness of His glory and the express image of His person...sat down at the right hand of the Majesty on high...."[2] God was revealing Himself through Jesus to the world, that "God speaks- He lives!"

There are other similarities between Jesus and Joseph. Both were objects of their father's love. Both were thirty years old when they began their ministries. Both were hated and betrayed by their brothers. Both were sold for pieces of silver. Both suffered for righteousness sake. Both were received and respected by gentiles. Both were married to gentile brides (Jesus' marriage is figurative of the gentile bride of the church). Both showed mercy and forgiveness to their brothers and enemies. And finally, both were saviors to Israel, having been exalted to the right hand of power.

Joseph: A Shadow of the Anti-Christ

At first glance, this concept of Joseph being a shadow of the Anti-Christ seems contradictory. How can Joseph be a picture of both Jesus and the Anti-Christ? The explanation is simple. Joseph provided for God's people during the seven-year famine, but the rest of the nations were brought into bondage under Pharaoh.

Consider these parallels between Joseph and the Anti-Christ. During Joseph's reign, all of Egypt (a type of the world) comes under Pharaoh's bondage. Plus, a seven-year tribulation of famine takes place, during which money fails, and all money comes under the dominion of Pharaoh. The people see Joseph as their savior and look to him as their source of sustenance.[3] Likewise, the Anti-Christ's seven-year tribulation includes the failure of money in which all look to him as a savior, for his ability to give sustenance and he brings the world into bondage under Satan. And God raised both men up to their places of power.

Finally, under Joseph the people of God do not come into bondage, but instead are blessed and provided for in Goshen. Likewise, the Christians do not come under the Anti-Christ's bondage, but live by faith and are blessed with God's provisions. The story of Joseph is a picture of the end times.

Joseph's Bad Report

> *"Joseph brought a bad report of his brothers to the father."*

While Joseph was feeding the flocks with his brothers, he noted their awful behavior. The Scriptures record, "Joseph brought a bad report of them to his father." Because Joseph was the favorite of their father and because of the bad report, his brothers, "Hated him and could not speak peaceably with him."[4]

> *Today it is the same. Carnal men do not want to hear about sin. They despise Christians who speak of receiving the favor of the Father by the forgiveness of sin.*

Today it is the same. Carnal men do not want to hear about sin. They despise Christians who speak of receiving the favor of the Father by the forgiveness of sin. As a result, carnal men ridicule and mock, "organized church", portray preachers as weak, and slam Christianity in their movie scripts and TV sitcoms.

Joseph's Two Dreams

Joseph told this dream to his family, "There we were binding sheaves in the field. Then behold, my sheaf arose and also stood upright; and indeed your sheaves stood all around and bowed down to my sheaf. And his brothers said to him, 'Shall you reign over us? Or shall you indeed have dominion over us?' So they hated him even more for his dreams and for his words."[5]

The dream is prophetic of the last days. A sheaf of wheat ultimately becomes bread. Jesus told his disciples to pray, "Give us this day, our daily bread."[6] True Christians acknowledge Jesus as their daily source of sustenance. But those who hate Him justify themselves with false wisdom such as, "God helps those who help themselves." These are the ones who will deny Jesus' dominion and will choose to accept the microchip identity.

Joseph dreamed a second time, "And this time, the sun, the moon, and the stars bowed down to me."[7] Note again the prophetic nature of the dream to the last days.

The sun, moon and stars are representative of the whole world bowing down to Joseph. In the end, the whole world will either bow to Jesus as disciples or they will bow to the Anti-Christ as golden calf adherents.

Ultimately, the golden calf crowd will discover the truth revealed in this scripture, "God also has highly exalted Him and given Him the name which is above every name, that at the name of Jesus every knee should bow, of those in heaven, and of those of the earth, and of those under the earth, and that every tongue should confess that Jesus Christ is Lord, to the glory of God the Father."[8]

Egyptian Slavery

The brothers were going to kill Joseph because of his bad report and dreams, but changed their minds and sold Joseph into slavery. They lied to their father Jacob by saying Joseph was torn to pieces by a wild beast. Eventually, Joseph ended up in Egypt as a servant to Potiphar. Because Potiphar's wife falsely accused Joseph of rape, he was put in prison.

In prison, he served as the administrator and had an opportunity to interpret the dreams of Pharaoh's two servants. One of the servants returned and when Pharaoh had a dream of his own, the servant told the ruler of Joseph's ability with dreams.

Pharaoh's Two Dreams

Genesis records this dialogue between Pharaoh and Joseph about the ruler's dream. "Suddenly seven cows came up out of the river, fine looking and fat; and they fed in the meadow. Then behold, seven other cows came up after them, poor and very ugly and gaunt, such ugliness, as I have never seen in all the land of Egypt. And the gaunt and ugly cows ate up the first seven, the fat cows...Also I saw in my dream...seven heads [grain] came up on one stalk, full and good. Then behold, seven heads, withered, thin, and blighted by the east wind, sprang up after them. And the thin heads devoured the seven good heads...Then Joseph said...God has shown Pharaoh what He is about to do. Indeed seven years of great plenty will come throughout all the land of Egypt; but after them seven years of famine will arise, and all the plenty will be forgotten in the land of Egypt; and the famine will deplete the land...the dream was repeated to Pharaoh twice because the thing is established by God, and God will shortly bring it to pass."[9]

> *"The gaunt and ugly cows ate up the fat cows"*

Remember in Part II? Cows were worshiped in ancient Egypt for their milk, cheese and meat. Here, the cows are combined with grain and were a divine indication of the nation's future famine. Joseph's solution was to gather the grain of the country during the good years to provide for the people during the seven-year famine.

The microchip identity is being created for the purpose of holding on to economic prosperity. Because of terrorism, identity fraud, and corruption, social architects are creating a system to continue the pursuit of economic freedom without hindrance. However, when the Anti-Christ causes the system to become mandatory by requiring the microchip, there will be a seven-year tribulation in which those who refuse the chip will not be able to buy or sell. Egypt's seven-year famine prevented plowing and harvesting and corresponds with the tribulation period of not being able to buy or sell.

Jesus, like Joseph has gone ahead of His brothers to prepare for what is about to happen in the world (Egypt). There is a season coming in which there will be no plowing and harvesting for the Christian, just like Joseph's time. Many reading this book may think they need to store provisions like Christians did during the Y2K scare. But they would be missing the point.

Jacob and his family did not prepare for the famine, the provisions were already prepared for them by God through Joseph. Proverbs says, "The wealth of the sinner is stored up for the righteous."[10] Hence, Jesus is preparing

> *"The wealth of the sinner is stored up for the righteous"*

for this season when our sheaves will bow down to His. He will provide for His brethren and all who will call upon His name during the time of the Anti-Christ's mandatory identity chip.

Joseph's Test

When the famine became severe, Jacob's sons went to Egypt to get bread. Upon seeing his brothers, Joseph set up a test. Jacob would not allow his youngest son Benjamin to go, lest some calamity should happen to him. Rachel, who was loved by Jacob, had born to him Benjamin and Joseph. Benjamin had now become Jacob's favorite son after the loss of Joseph. The test was centered on the brothers' attitude toward Benjamin and to determine if they were honest men.

Joseph's identity was not recognized because he had grown up in Egypt and his appearance had drastically changed with the Egyptian culture. Joseph gave the brothers the grain, but accused them of being spies. In their defense, they told Joseph about their family,

Benjamin, and Jacob. Joseph demanded they leave one brother named Simeon as collateral, until they returned with Benjamin as proof they were telling the truth.

The brothers were grieved as they discerned the present distress was a judgment from God. They said to one another, "We are truly guilty concerning our brother [Joseph], for we saw the anguish of his soul when he pleaded with us, and we would not hear; Therefore this distress has come upon us…his blood is now required of us. But they did not know that Joseph understood them."[11] The brothers returned home with the grain, but without Simeon.

Eventually their grain was depleted and they returned, bringing with them Benjamin. Judah swore to his father Jacob, he would make sure nothing happened to the child. Joseph continued the test by giving his brothers the grain they ask for, but put his personal drinking cup in the sack of grain belonging to Benjamin. Once they had departed, Joseph sent his servants after them to take as prisoner the one with whom the cup was found.

The brothers were dismayed and refused to leave without Benjamin, because of the grief it would bring to Jacob. Judah insisted that he be substituted as a prisoner for Benjamin. At this point, Joseph realized his brothers had truly repented and revealed himself to them. Joseph, proclaimed, "God sent me before you to preserve a posterity for you in the earth, and to save your lives by a great deliverance."[12]

The Test Results

> *The brothers asked an important question, "What is this that God has done to us?"*

In getting the grain and enduring the test, the brothers asked one another an important question, "What is this that God has done to us?"[13] The question seems to ponder, is this seven year famine a blessing or a curse? In the same way Christians will ask, "Is God's end time test of the microchip identity, a blessing or a curse?"

Had it not been for the famine, Jacob's sons would have been content to live in their backslidden condition. They would not have been motivated to deal with their past sin. But because of the famine,

> *Is God's end time test of the microchip identity, a blessing or a curse?*

they were confronted with the same temptation to betray Benjamin as they had Joseph, for their own welfare. They could have betrayed Benjamin and continued to grieve their father Jacob. But they came to repentance and were willing to lay down their lives for the sake of their father's conscience.

It is the same with the microchip identity. These last days will reveal every man's heart and confront him with his carnality. Many individuals have rejected Jesus for various reasons and grieved the Father's heart. The individual can accept the microchip identity and continue to grieve the Father's heart or they can repent and embrace the divine provisions of Jesus.

> *God's purpose is to force every man to make a definitive decision about Jesus before His final judgments are executed.*

To understand the test of the microchip identity and ignore the Father's heart by accepting the chip is to betray your family, friends, and co-workers for covetous pursuits. Or, you can refuse the chip and come to the Lordship of Jesus with a humble and broken heart, acknowledging your need for the Savior's sustenance. God's purpose is to force every man to make a definitive decision about Jesus before His final judgments are executed.

The Provider's Provisions

When the brothers returned to Jacob, they exclaimed, "Joseph is still alive, and he is governor over all the land of Egypt. And Jacob's heart stood still, because he did not believe them...but when he saw the carts which Joseph had sent to carry him, the spirit

> *"Joseph is still alive, and he is governor over all the land of Egypt. And Jacob's heart stood still..."*

of Jacob revived."[14] The first great provision of God for these last days is that *Jesus is alive and Lord of all the earth.* People believe the church is dead, but the prophetic word proves God is alive and in control to carry Christians to safety.

Secondly, during the famine Joseph provided his brothers with grain out of favor, unlike the Egyptians who had to pay. Joseph proclaimed, "God sent me before you to preserve life."[15] When Christians are no longer able to buy and sell because they have refused the microchip identity, Jesus will continue to provide their "daily bread." The Scriptures promise, "Let your conduct be without covetousness; be content with such things as you have. For He Himself has said, 'I will never leave you nor forsake you.' So we may boldly say: The Lord is my helper; I will not fear. What can man do to me?"[16]

> *"God sent me before you to preserve life"*
> *-Joseph*

Third, Joseph gave his family Goshen. He said, "You shall dwell in the land of Goshen...there I will provide for you...I will give you the best of the land of Egypt, and you will eat the fat of the land."[17] The Egyptians were losing everything they had. They gave up their money, their land and finally their bodies for bread. Pharaoh owned their souls as they tried to hold on to their lives. But God's people were being blessed.

This story of Joseph is a picture of the last days. Consider the words of Jesus, "Whoever desires to come after Me, let him deny himself, and take up his cross, and follow Me. For whoever desires to save his life will lose it, but whoever loses his life for My sake and the gospel's will save it. For what will it profit a man if he gains the whole world, and loses his own soul? Or what will a man give in exchange for his soul? For whoever is ashamed of Me and My words in this adulterous generation, of him the Son of Man also will be ashamed when He comes in the glory of His Father with the holy angels."[18] The Egyptians gave everything to Pharaoh in an effort to hold onto their lives and lost their souls. Christians will lose their lives (current way of living) but save their souls because they trust in Jesus.

Finally, God gave Jacob a wonderful promise. If Jacob would trust Joseph, God said, "I will go down with you to Egypt, and I will surely bring you up again."[19] The Christian will surely need to trust Jesus in these last days when he will no longer be able to buy or sell. As the apostle said, "The just shall live by faith."[20] But God gives a sure promise; He will bring the Christian up again. Hallelujah!

Summary

The story of Joseph is a magnificent picture of Jesus in the last days. It is a picture of a loving God restoring backslidden brothers by calling them to repentance and covering them with love, mercy and provision.

Joseph proclaimed, "You meant evil against me; but God meant it for good, in order to bring it about as it is this day, to save many people alive. Now therefore, do not be afraid; I will provide for you and your little ones. And he comforted them and spoke kindly to them."[21] As Joseph was to his brothers, so Jesus is to you and I, be encouraged.

Fifteen

"Don't Give Me Your Bull!" – God

"For it is not possible that the blood of bulls…
could take away sins."   Hebrews 10:4

The business world is notorious for using a sales pitch called the "bait and switch." The principle is simple. The promotion expounds the magnificence of the offer. Once the customer decides to buy, he is given something inferior. If the customer discovers the switch, the businessman simply smiles and pacifies. Satan does the same thing in deceiving mankind with the microchip identity. His offer appears appetizing. But once you "Get Chipped", he just smiles, rejoicing in the deception.

Adam and Eve's Clothes

When Adam and Eve sinned and discovered their nakedness, God made "tunics of skin, and clothed them." The skins were a much better covering than the flimsy fig leaves of their own devising. The skins required the shedding of an animal's innocent blood. This was a prophetic picture of God's plan *for salvation* called, "The

Book of Life of the Lamb slain from the foundation of the world."[1]

When Adam and Eve's children brought offerings, the sacrifices reflected their heart attitudes. Abel was a shepherd and brought the fat of an innocent lamb. His offering was an acknowledgement of his understanding that God through mercy, had provided forgiveness of sins, just has He had done for his parents, by the shedding of innocent blood. Cain's offering was the fruit of the ground that he had tilled, by the sweat of his brow and the skill of his hands.

"Am I my brother's keeper?" God accepted Abel's offering, but rejected Cain's. Abel's offering reflected appreciation for what God had done for him, whereas Cain's offering reflected what he had done for God. In the end, Cain became angry and killed Abel. And when God came asking where Abel was, Cain rudely replied, "I do not know. Am I my brother's keeper?"[2] Yes, we are our brother's keeper. For this reason Cain was cursed, given a mark, and sent out from the presence of God.

Don't Give Me Your Bull!

The same night the death angel took the life of Egypt's first born, the children of Israel killed the Passover lamb as a reminder of God's mercy *to deliver* by the shedding of innocent blood. When the Hebrew offered animal sacrifices during their wanderings in the desert, it was again a reminder of God's grace *to provide* in the wilderness by the shedding of innocent blood.

Over the course of time, the Israelites lost sight of what the animal sacrifice meant. They lost the understanding that the shed blood of the innocent life represented God's clothing them with *salvation, deliverance and provision.*

The worship of the golden calf was the worship of the creature, rather than the Creator. The backslidden heart saw the cow as its source of sustenance more than God. This attitude carried over into worship, as they offered the animal sacrifice. Their offering became a prideful laying down of a portion of their prosperity to show God what good people they were with the hope that God would approve, much like Cain's sacrifice.

God was not pleased with this distortion, as this Scripture attests, "To what purpose is the multitude of your sacrifices to Me? I have had enough of burnt offerings of rams and the fat of cattle. I do not delight in the blood of

> *God is not interested in the cow, He is interested in the heart*

lambs or goats. When you come to appear before Me, who has required this from your hand, to trample My courts?"[3] God is not interested in the cow; He is interested in the heart. He is not interested in what one gives, but how one responds to what He has already given.

The Acceptable Sacrifice

King David understood this truth when he came to God with repentance for his sins. David cried, "Create in me a clean heart, O God, and renew a steadfast spirit within me...restore to me the joy of Your salvation, and uphold me by Your generous Spirit...For You do not desire sacrifice, or else I would give it; You do not delight in burnt offering. The sacrifices of God are a broken spirit, a broken and a contrite heart, These, O God, You will not despise."[4]

God is looking for relationship, not sacrifice. He desires a people who are grateful for *salvation, deliverance and provision.* A people who understand that God has provided everything from the foundation of the world.

John the Baptist understood this truth. He looked upon Jesus and cried out, "Behold the Lamb of God who takes away the sin of the world!"[5] He understood that Jesus' blood was the heavenly fulfillment of the earthly animal sacrifice, extending *salvation, deliverance and provision* for mankind.

Christians are encouraged to remember Abel's attitude of gratefulness. The Scripture says, "Therefore by Him [Jesus] let us continually offer the sacrifice of praise to God, that is, the fruit of our lips, giving thanks to His name."[6] Genuine Christians understand God's provisions as set forth in the Bible, "Blessed be the God and Father of our Lord Jesus Christ, who has blessed us with every spiritual blessing in Christ."[7] The Christian's sacrifices are from the spirit. Like Abel, their inner man's adores, worships, and magnifies God for what He has done for them.

The New Pharisees

The Pharisees held fast to traditions, even when they violated the will of God. Because of those traditions, they viewed themselves as superior to their fellowman. Jesus said of them, "You also outwardly appear righteous to men, but inside you are full of hypocrisy and lawlessness."[8] Today's golden calf crowd does the same. They hold fast to politically correct speech and attitudes in the name of social conformity, even though it violates

God's Word. Those viewpoints are held in respect for the esteem of their peers, not God.

The Apostle Paul wrote, "If anyone...does not consent...to the Words of our Lord Jesus Christ...he is proud, knowing nothing, but is obsessed with disputes and arguments over words...useless wranglings of men of corrupt minds and destitute of the truth, who suppose that godliness is a means of gain. From such withdraw yourself."[9]

The golden calf crowd clings to a "form of godliness but denying its power." They claim, "In God We Trust", but do they really? This religious form expresses itself in all manner of charities in an attempt to find society's approval.

> *The golden calf crowd clings to a "form of godliness but denying its power." They claim, "In God We Trust", but do they really?*

Superstar athletes, movie stars, recording artists, and corporations all have charities that bolster their reputation to the community. Unfortunately, they are wasted offerings just like Cain's. Why? Because the offering glorifies the giver, not God.

Jesus noted, "For whoever gives you a cup of water to drink in My name, because you belong to Christ, assuredly, I say to you, he will by no means lose his reward."[10] The charities of the golden calf crowd are not done in the honor of Jesus, nor gratefulness for salvation, but instead for the appearance of goodness, and eventual economic gain. This form of religion, though it benefits the community is a waste because of its selfish exaltation.

Our Brother's Keeper

The golden calf crowd will proclaim the many benefits of the microchip identity. They will glow over its ability to diminish terrorism. They will shout about its conveniences. But, this is a deceptive "bait and switch." The microchip identity is not founded on what God has done for man, but what man's ingenuity can do for God.

The social architects are developing the microchip identity under the banner of, "In God We Trust." However, God prohibits the system they are building. The microchip identity betrays the Christian who cannot accept the "mark of the beast" for conscious sake. Though the fruit of the Christian's labor is from God, Satan seeks through the microchip identity to "kill, steal and destroy" the Christian's ability to enjoy life.

> *The social architects are developing the microchip identity under the banner of, "In God We Trust." But the system betrays the Christian who cannot accept the "mark of the beast" for conscious sake*

> *Cain refused to be his brother's keeper and because of this attitude, Cain was marked by God and sent out from His presence*

Cain refused to be his brother's keeper and because of this attitude, Cain was marked by God and sent out from His presence. Likewise, the golden calf crowd will be marked with the microchip identity and sent out from God. For the Scriptures declare, "And the smoke of their torment ascends forever and ever; and they have no rest day or night, who worship the beast and his image, and whoever receives the mark of his name. Here is the patience of the saints; here are those who keep the commandments of God and the faith of Jesus."[11]

Aaron's Weakness

This "bait and switch" spirit even infiltrates the church. The masses are disillusioned with church, as they perceive the institution is all about money. It is a feeling that the church is dependent upon the people, not the people upon God. As a result, good people leave fed up with the constant pleas for more money. They walk in confusion pondering what the church stands for or its purpose in the community. How did this happen? The answer is with Aaron.

Moses confronted Aaron about making the people a golden calf. Moses said to Aaron, "What did this people do to you that you have brought so great a sin upon them?" and Aaron replied, "They said to me, 'Make us gods that shall go before us; as for this Moses, the man who brought us out of the land of Egypt, we do not know what has become of him.' And I said to them, 'Whoever has any gold, let him break it off and they gave it to me, and I cast it into the fire, and the calf came out." The Scripture concludes, "Moses saw that the people where unrestrained (for Aaron had not restrained them, to their shame)."[12] Several questions are answered in this passage.

What did the people do? They longed for a different god, one that would express their carnal yearnings because they were confused about Moses (Christ) coming. What did Aaron the priest do? He accommodated them by taking up offerings of gold. He made for them the golden calf that expressed their carnal appetites. Instead of restraining the people, he gave them what they wanted. In the process, he became the embodiment of that carnal spirit. Notice, they gave the gold to Aaron, not to God.

Today, people are frustrated with the excesses of carnal preachers. Their sermons are centered on giving more...and more...and more. The carnal preacher has become the expression of what the world yearns for because he has accommodated their covetous spirit in the manner of Aaron.

This is the spirit the Apostle Paul warned about, "For the time will come when they will not endure sound doctrine, but according to their own desires, because they have itching ears, they will heap up for themselves teachers; and they will turn their ears away from the truth, and be turned aside to fables. But you be watchful in all things, endure afflictions..."[13]

What the Church Needs Today

The church needs men of God who will restrain the people from their covetous appetites, exhorting the saints to faith and patience. This takes spiritual character and moral backbone. The church needs reassurance that although Christ may be delayed, He is coming and in the meantime has provided everything the Christian needs for the wilderness journey.

When the church understands with full assurance that God has provided *salvation, deliverance and provision*, saints will bring their offerings with cheerful hearts. Those offerings will be given with the right motive of thanksgiving in the spirit of Abel. And God "loves a cheerful giver."

The church needs to come out of its shame. Our nation is divided and our churches are divided. Christianity is not about our wealth, our prosperity, or us. It is about God's magnificent *salvation, deliverance and provision* for all who trust in Him. I long to see the people of God returning to sanctuaries, filling them with thunderous praise for God's magnificent gifts.

Personal Testimonies

When I was young and considering marriage, the thought of providing for a wife seemed overwhelming. The same concern grew when my wife informed me of being pregnant with our first child. Each of our six children has been a step of faith.

The apprehensions dissolved one night when my second child was born. The same apprehensions were tormenting me once again, "How am I going to provide for this child?" In the wee hours of the morning, the nurses handed me the infant to hold while they took my wife to a room. While I was pondering the awesome wonder of the newborn child, the presence of God came into the delivery room. God spoke to me in a clear voice, "I will never give you one that I will not provide for." Suddenly, there was a reassurance of God's faithfulness. That God was not only the source of life, but my provider in life too. Everyone needs this revelation as the microchip identity unfolds.

"I will never give you a child that I will not provide for"-God

Throughout the years, my inner man has struggled with believing God for his provisions. The human tendency has been to wrestle with God, seeking to provide in my own strength and then relenting, crying out to God for His help. And I have discovered whenever I pray with all my heart, God comes running with the answers.

One such occasion had to do with providing my family with a home. Our family was growing and we had three children in one bedroom and another on the way. One bedroom was filled with storage and the 900 square foot home was cramped. I found myself in the woods in back of our home each evening crying out to God for a bigger home. "One we can afford without decades of debt," I prayed. After several weeks of fervent prayer, God brought the answer.

One Saturday morning I was awakened by a noise next door. With a cup of coffee in hand, I watched house movers jacked up my neighbor's house. The land underneath had surpassed the value of the house itself. My neighbor had sold the land and the house was being moved to make room for a commercial building. The movers explained to me they had bought the house for a few thousand dollars.

Suddenly, God had presented me with an opportunity. I could do the same thing. Immediately, my wife and I began to bid on homes to be moved. After some months, we successfully bought a much larger house for a few thousand dollars. The problem was, we didn't have any land.

I looked at a lot and called the number on the "for sale" sign. The sign said $28,000.00 in 1988. "Hello", said the stranger. I explained to the man I wanted to come make an offer on the land. "Let me save you the trip", the man replied, "Just tell me the offer over the phone." I was prepared to pay the full asking price; after all I had a house but no land. But God prompted me to say, "I want the land at $18,000.00." The landowner stuttered and hesitantly said, "Well...come on over I suppose." I promptly filled out the necessary paper work and went to visit the owner.

The owner called his wife into the kitchen and looked over the paperwork. He then smiled and confessed, "I told my wife this morning if God sent someone today with an offer for exactly $18,000.00, I would sell the land. I am a man of my word, the land is yours." Hallelujah! God provided every step of the way.

The Soap Provision

> *God must have laughed at our simple faith*

When my wife and I where first married, we committed ourselves to giving thanksgiving offerings to the Lord on a regular basis. On one such evening we had gone to the grocery store before going to church. When the groceries were tallied at the cash register, we both realized we could not buy everything and still give our offering. So we put the bars of soap back on the shelf. After all, one can always stretch those slivers a few more showers, we thought. God must have laughed at our simple faith.

I was a sales-rep for a corrugated box company at the time. The very next day as I was traveling my territory, I noticed a new company. The businessman explained he was importing expensive French soap and needed boxes. After striking a deal, he asked, "Would you like some free samples?" "Of course!" I exuded. That day he gave me a cardboard box full of sweet smelling French soap to take home to my wife. And every time I visited, he would send me home with more soap. We constantly had soap and not just any soap; it was an aroma fit for royalty. Oh how we laughed with glee at the humor of God.

> *Oh how we laughed with glee at the humor of God*

Then our Pastor sent us to another state to plant a church. One day as I was passing out tracts at the fairgrounds, an older couple walked up and asked if they could help. Soon they began attending the church. One day I asked them where they worked. "Oh, we both work in a soap factory," they replied. "Would you like some soap," he inquired? The amazing thing was; we had just run out of the French soap. God blessed our family with soap and shampoo for over a decade.

Summary

God provides more than soap. He extends *salvation, deliverance and provision* to everyone. And He does not discriminate between good and evil. His love is unconditional. The scriptures says, "He makes His sun rise on the evil and on the good, and sends rain on the just and on the unjust."[14] The Bible declares, "For God so loved the world that He gave His only begotten Son, that whoever believes in Him should not perish but have everlasting life."[15] Whoever is whoever! His blessings are for everyone.

Today, people need reassurance. America is divided between living for God and living for self. But only God can satisfy the soul. Striving for the world's approval is the shameful covering of one's nakedness with fig leaves. No amount of living politically correct lives, conforming to society, or giving to a charity will ever make God love you anymore than when the Lamb of God was slain before the foundation of the world. God has already provided better coats of skin in the death and resurrection of Jesus Christ.

Like Cain and Abel, we must choose between living with grateful hearts, trusting in the *salvation, deliverance and provisions* of God or the efforts of self to produce fruit acceptable to God. Our response should be that of thanksgiving in the spirit of Abel.

Sixteen

The Last Golden Calf

*"If anyone worships the beast and his image, and
receives his mark...He shall be tormented with fire and
brimstone...And the smoke of their torment ascends
forever and ever; and they have no rest day or night, who
worship the beast and his image, and whoever receives
the mark of his name. Here is the patience of the saints;
here are those who keep the commandments of God and
the faith of Jesus." Revelation 14:9-12*

The terrorist bombing of the twin towers has changed
America forever. Before the bombings, social architects
struggled to get a platform to share their utopian ideas for
the microchip identity. Now, their ideas are being openly
discussed on the evening news. America is searching for
answers to bring more security to its citizens. Even
conservative talk show hosts are discussing the trade-off
of civil liberty to embrace some form of national
identification. Suddenly, many corporations which were
hush-hush about developing microchip implants for
human identification are shouting "me too."

As I write this chapter, the local news just announced
Hitachi Corporation has a microchip, the size of a grain

of sand and can be used for identification and commerce.[1] Recently over lunch, an IBM executive shared a new product soon to be announced. "We have implantable barcodes that will fit on the head of a pin", he tells me. They are invisible to the naked eye and fit under the skin for identification and commerce.

Suddenly, many corporations which were hush-hush about developing microchip implants for human identification are shouting "me too."

Microchip ingenuity is the latest version of man's invention called money, an idea that men have come to trust. Money's evolution has gone from cattle, to precious metals, to coins, to paper, to plastic, and now to a microchip to be implanted under the skin.

Regardless of the invention's form, when abused, "The love of money is the root of all evil: which while some coveted after, they have erred from the faith, and pierced themselves through with many sorrows."[2] This latest monetary expression will cause mankind to choose either the Anti-Christ or God.

Where Satan Dwells?

Jesus spoke of a city called Pergamos, "Where Satan's throne is...where Satan dwells." [3] There, people held the doctrine of Balaam. Of course Balaam was an example of those who compromised God for the love of money. History records the significance of Pergamos. "Rome defeated Pergamum in 133 B.C. and became the chief town of Asia, and the site of *the first* temple of the Caesar-cult, erected to Rome and [Caesar] Augustus in 29 B.C."[4]

Theologian M.J.S. Rudwich, Ph.D. explains the city's spiritual climate. "Pergamum was seen as the seat of the power of evil because in the imperial cult, the God-given power of the State had been harnessed to the blasphemous worship of a man. Worship of the emperor had been made the touchstone of civic loyalty, so that a faithful Christian, however loyal to the secular authority of the State, was branded as a traitor."[5]

"Pergamenian coins illustrated the importance which the community attached to this cult. Caracella [a political figure] is shown on one coin, saluting a serpent...[and] on the crag above

> *"A faithful Christian, however loyal to the secular authority of the State, was branded as a traitor"*

Pergamum was a throne-like altar to Zeus...Zeus to deepen Christian horror at Pergamum's obsession with the serpent-image, was called in this connection, 'Zeus the Savior.'"[6] This coin can be seen in the museum of Berlin.

"The Lie"

The Caesar-cult money reflecting the worship of both man and creature is finding new expression in the microchip identity. The worship of money is as old as cow worship. Cattle are the oldest known form of wealth. Cows were worshipped for their milk, cheese, meat and ability to give sustenance to mankind. The cow's reverence is seen throughout history from the ancient Taurus of astrology, to flower adorned Hindu cows, and the optimistic Wall Street bull.

The Apostle Paul refers to the foolishness of cow worship as "the lie". He said, "Professing themselves to be wise, they became fools, and changed the glory of the incorruptible God into an image made like corruptible man...and four-footed animals...Therefore God gave them up…who exchanged the truth of God for the lie, and worshiped and served the creature rather than the Creator."[7]

The Prophet Isaiah spoke of carving wood and overlaying it with gold to make an idol, like the golden calf image, as stupidity. He prophetically declares, "He falls down before it and worships it, prays

> *"Is there not a lie in my right hand?"*
> *-Isaiah*

to it and says, 'Deliver me, for you are my god!'… And no one considers in his heart, nor is there knowledge nor understanding to say… 'Shall I fall down before a block of wood?'… a deceived heart has turned him aside; and he cannot deliver his soul, nor say, 'Is there not a lie in my right hand?'" [8]

Paul again referred to *"the lie"* in reference to the Anti-Christ. He said, "The coming of the lawless one is according to the working of Satan, with all power, signs, and lying wonders, and with all unrighteous deception among those who perish, because they did not receive the love of the truth, that they might be saved. And for this reason God will send them strong delusion, that they should believe the lie, that they all may be condemned who did not believe the truth but had pleasure in unrighteousness."[9] Covetous pleasure has laid the foundation for the arrival of the Anti-Christ and his mark.

> *"The lie" deceives the human heart into believing the microchip identity, like the cow, is mankind's source of sustenance*

"The lie" deceived the human heart into worshipping the cow as mankind's source of sustenance. *"The lie"* is again deceiving the human heart into worshipping the Anti-Christ's microchip identity, as the only way to survive and maintain one's lifestyle of pleasure. *The Last Golden Calf is The Microchip Identity.*

Covetousness Divides a Nation

Even Israel, like the pagan nations succumbed to worshipping the golden calf when Moses delayed in his coming. Many years later, the ancient cult worship resurrected itself again, first in the lifestyle of King Solomon and then in Israel. The golden calf image was erected by Jeroboam to split the kingdom and keep the people from going to God's temple. Each succeeding king continued the abomination until the people of God were destroyed as a nation.

Today the spirit of covetousness is affecting America in the same way. Our nation is divided and suffering a spiritual civil war. No outside enemy can threaten her stability as the most powerful nation on earth. But the spirit of covetousness is eating away at her moral strength. This weakness is causing a people who pledged, "One nation under God, indivisible," to follow the example of Israel's division and downfall.

The ingenuity of the very people who claim "In God We Trust" are laying the monetary foundation that will be used by the Anti-Christ to destroy the Christian's freedom to participate in the economy and at the same time be obedient to God.

This covetous spirit can be seen in the writings of President Abraham Lincoln during the darkest days of the civil war, a previous time when our nation was divided. Below is an excerpt of Lincoln's proclamation for a national day of prayer and fasting.

A Proclamation:

And whereas it is the duty of nations
as well as of men, to owe their dependence

upon the overruling power of God, to confess their sins and transgressions, in humble sorrow, yet with assured hope that genuine repentance will lead to mercy and pardon; and to recognize the sublime truth, announced in the Holy Scriptures and proven by all history, that those nations only are blessed whose God is the Lord.

And, insomuch as we know that, by His divine law, nations like individuals are subjected to punishments and chastisements in this world, may we not justly fear that the awful calamity of civil war, which now desolates the land, may be but a punishment, inflicted upon us, for our presumptuous sins, the needful end of our national reformation as a whole People? We have been the recipients of the choicest bounties of Heaven. We have been preserved, these many years, in peace and prosperity. We have grown in numbers, wealth and power, as no other nation has ever grown. But we have forgotten God. We have forgotten the gracious hand which preserved us in peace, and multiplied and enriched and strengthened us; and we have vainly imagined, in the deceitfulness of our hearts, that all these blessings were produced by some superior wisdom and virtue of our own. Intoxicated with unbroken success, we have become too self-sufficient to feel the necessity of redeeming and preserving grace, too proud to pray to the God that made us!

It behooves us then, to humble ourselves before the offended Power, to confess our national sins, and to pray for clemency and forgiveness....

All this being done, in sincerity and truth, let us then rest humbly in the hope authorized by the Divine teachings, that the united cry of the Nation will be heard on high, and answered with blessing, no less than the pardon of our national sins, and the restoration of our now divided and suffering Country, to its former happy condition and unity of peace.

> *Intoxicated with unbroken success, we have become too self-sufficient to feel the necessity of redeeming and preserving grace, too proud to pray to the God that made us!*
> *-Abe Lincoln*

President Abraham Lincoln

Yes, America is divided once again. The war for her soul is between those who focus on money as their source and those desiring godly balance. The civil war resulted in the physical death of many as they sought to deliver the country from slavery. Today's civil war will result in the spiritual death of many if the country is not delivered from its slavery to covetousness.

What Remains is More Glorious!

As America succumbs to the covetous spirit and implements the microchip identity, God has assured individual saints of provision through our Joseph-Jesus. Our faithful God has already provided temporal provision and spiritual destiny for those who reject the identity chip and walk by faith.

But the fate of our nation rests in the willingness of Christians to pray and repent. God made a sovereign promise, "If My people who are called by My name will humble themselves, and pray and seek My face, and turn from their wicked [covetous] ways, then I will hear from heaven, and will forgive their sin and heal their land."[10] If Christians *will* obey, God *will* heal America.

Our Christian communities must set the example. Christians must consistently honor the seventh day of creation. They must restore the priority of family, recover a balanced work ethic, and Christians must pray for God's mercy to our nation.

Christians are called to emulate Christ. Jesus demonstrated dominion by laying down His life. He recognized the Father's kingdom was not of this world. Jesus did not come to be a king, living in fancy castles with luxurious furnishings, but to bring the knowledge of salvation. Likewise, Christians must lay down the pursuit of materialism as their first priority and live modestly, not in financial slavery, but serving others in the knowledge of Christ.

> *This spiritual character is a solid witness worthy of the banner, "In God We Trust."*

What remains is more glorious! A revived nation will be a glowing example to the rest of the world. Balanced living brings restored churches, families, and work ethics. This spiritual character is a solid witness worthy of the banner, "In God We Trust."

You Have to Believe!

In championship games, television cameras scan the audience to show fans passionately rooting for their team. Often the fans of an underdog team will have signs proclaiming, "You have to believe!" Jesus said, "I have told you before it comes, that when it comes to pass, you may believe."[11] Believing is a choice girded up by prophecy and reality. To fans of Jesus I say, "You have to believe."

The last book of the Bible begins with, "The Revelation of Jesus Christ, which God gave Him to show His servants, things which must shortly take place." [12] God keeps the saints informed so they can prepare for the future revealing of Jesus.

Jesus encouraged the saints, "Because you have kept My command to persevere, I also will keep you from the hour of trial which shall come upon the whole world, to test those who dwell on the earth."[13] Tests are passed or failed. Those who study and prepare usually pass, but those who are lazy usually fail. This spiritual test is centered on the microchip identity being implemented by social architects.

> *"Because you have kept My command to persevere, I also will keep you from the hour of trial which shall come upon the whole world, to test those who dwell on the earth." -Jesus*

Two thousand years ago, the Apostle John wrote about this test. Jesus told John, "And authority was given him [the Anti-Christ] over every tribe, tongue and nation.... He causes all, both small and great, rich and poor, free and slave, to receive a mark on their right hand or on their forehead, and that no one may buy or sell except one who has the mark..."[14]

When in the history of man have we bought and sold with anything other than cash or barter? It has only been since the mid-nineteen fifties that money took the form of plastic and only in recent years that plastic has begun to transition from magnetic strips to microchips to be implanted in the hand.

Summary

The microchip identity would merely be another plateau in the evolution of money if it were not for the judgment pronounced on those who receive it. The Apostle John records, "If anyone worships the beast and his image, and receives his mark…He shall be tormented with fire and brimstone…And the smoke of their torment ascends forever and ever; and they have no rest day or night, who worship the beast and his image, and whoever receives the mark of his name. Here is the patience of the saints; here are those who keep the commandments of God and the faith of Jesus."[15]

God rejects the mark. Its implantation is an acknowledgment of the Anti-Christ as one's source of sustenance. It is the same spirit of the golden calf, worshipping the creature for its milk, cheese, and meat.

The splashing of cow urine on one's face and drinking the ammonia-spiked fluid is lunacy, no matter how reverently it is done. It is worshipping the creature more than the Creator. Likewise, the microchip identity is the worship of man's ingenuity more than God. To lose one's salvation over misplaced trust is crazy.

The golden calf is a lesson in the duplicity of the human heart. The Prophet Jeremiah said, "The heart is deceitful above all things, and desperately wicked; who can know it? I, the Lord, search the heart, I test the mind…he who gets riches, but not by right…at his end he will be a fool." [16] This is the ultimate mad cow disease.

If one can place faith in a cow, one can trust the Lord. If one can place faith in a microchip, one can trust God. Which will you trust? Which will be the object of your faith? What decision will you make? Will you be a fool, or will you be a man or woman of God?

Without the ability to buy and sell, Christians will definitely need the faith and patience of Jesus as they transition into a new lifestyle of living modestly in the service of God, family and community. Are you ready to believe? Are you ready to commit yourself to the Lordship of Jesus Christ? Are you ready for revival?

If so, follow the words of James. "Therefore be patient, brethren, until the coming of the Lord. See how the farmer waits for the precious fruit of the earth, waiting patiently for it until it receives the early and latter rain. You also be patient. Establish your hearts, for the coming of the Lord is at hand."[17]

How Biochips Communicate

A biochip for implantation is also known as a radio-frequency identification device (RFID) and sends a signal to a scanner, which reveals an identification number to a computer database. This is how it works.

Biochip transponders are about the size of a grain of rice. The components are sealed in a tiny tube made of soda lime glass, which is known for tissue compatibility, ensuring zero risk of infection or tissue rejection. The tube is sealed so that body fluids cannot reach the internal mechanisms.

The biochip has three elements. First, a silicon chip receives a laser etched ID number. Secondly, a coil of copper wire is wound tightly around a small ferrite (iron) core rod and serves as an antenna to communicate information. The antenna also receives useful energy from the radio frequency wave to energize itself, and therefore has no battery and does not wear out. And third, a capacitor holds the energy. The radio wave is a low frequency 125 kHz signal that penetrates all objects, except those made of metal.

Endnotes:

Preface
[1] John 16:1-2
[2] Amos 3:7
[3] First Corinthians 10:11
[4] First Thessalonians 5:21
[5] First Corinthians 13:12
[6] Daniel 12:9
[7] Jeremiah 23:20
[8] Matthew 24:42
[9] Revelation 1:1
[10] Revelation 3:3
[11] Matthew 16:2-3

One: Man's Amazing Ingenuity: Money
[1] Revelation 13:16-17
[2] Revelation 14:9-11
[3] Hebrews 13:5
[4] Genesis 13:2 KJV
[5] Job 1:3
[6] Genesis 24:22
[7] Joshua 7:21
[8] National Geographic, January 1993, Article titled "The Power of Money" pg.88
[9] Exodus 20:4 KJV
[10] The New Bible Dictionary, Inter-Varsity Fellowship 1962, "Money" pgs. 836-841
[11] Exodus 20:5
[12] Exodus 20:4
[13] John 4:24
[14] National Geographic, January 1993, Article titled "The Power of Money" pg.91
[15] National Geographic, January 1993, Article titled "The Power of Money" pg.84
[16] The World Book Encyclopedia, Field Enterprises Educational Corp. 1959, pg.2508
[17] The World Book Encyclopedia, Field Enterprises Educational Corp. 1959, pg. 8364

One Continued: Man's Amazing Ingenuity: Money
[18] The World Book Encyclopedia, Field Enterprises Educational Corp. 1959, pg. 5183
[19] ibid
[20] The World Book Encyclopedia, Field Enterprises Educational Corp. 1959, pg. 5184
[21] ibid
[22] The World Book Encyclopedia, Field Enterprises Educational Corp. 1959, pg. 2507
[23] National Geographic, January 1993, Article titled "The Power of Money" pg.92
[24] Proverbs 22:7
[25] Time Magazine, Article titled "The Big Bank Theory and What it says about The Future of Money" April 27, 1998 Vol. 151 NO. 16
[26] ibid
[27] Website date 6/26/01 www.mondexphil.com/default.htm
[28] Isaiah 41:23 // 43:9-11 // 45:21-22 // 46:9-10 // 48:3-5
[29] Revelation 13:16-17
[30] Revelation 14:10-11
[31] Mark 8:36
[32] Revelation 18:13, 23

Two: The Microchip Identity's Evolution
[1] Raleigh News and Observer, June 23, 1992 article: "Stripes Make a Star of Raleigh Inventor"
[2] Article by Elaine M. Ramesh called "Time Enough? Consequences of Human Microchip Implantation, www.fplc.edu/risk/vol8/fall/ramesh.htm
[3] Hosea 4:6
[4] Article by Terry L. Cook, titled "America's Identity Crisis and Coming National I.D. Chip", www.worthynews.com/Government/chip.htm
[5] "Digital Angel: The New Eye in the Sky" www.foxnews.com/vtech/101600/da.sml
[6] 'Digital Angel' set to fly tomorrow, www.worldnetdaily.com/news/article.asp?ARTICLE-ID=23232
[7] ibid
[8] Time Magazine, Article titled "The Big Bank Theory and What it says about The Future of Money" April 27, 1998 Vol. 151 NO. 16

[9] 'Digital Angel' set to fly tomorrow,
www.worldnetdaily.com/news/article.asp?ARTICLE-ID=23232
[10] ibid
[11] ibid
[12] CHRISTIAN MEDIA – Dec. 31, 2001 Copyright ©2001 Christian Media Network
[13] CBS News.com Article, "Finding the Bad Guys", February 10th, 2002
[14] Washington Post Staff Writer, Saturday, November 3, 2001
[15] "YOUR PAPERS, PLEASE ..." By Sherrie Gossett© 2002 WorldNetDaily.com
[16] ibid
[17] ibid
[18] "Injectable chip opens door to 'human bar code'" By Charles J. Murray, January 6, 2002
[19] Applied Digital Solutions' Press Release dated April 4th, 2002
[20] Applied Digital Solutions' Press Release dated April 22nd, 2002
[21] Your Papers Please...Post 9/11 Security Fears Usher in Subdermal Chips, by Sherrie Gossett © 2002 WorldNetDaily.com
[22] Proverbs 22:3

Three: The Microchip Economy is Here!

[1] Time Magazine, Article titled "The Big Bank Theory and What it says about The Future of Money" April 27, 1998 Vol. 151 NO. 16
[2] ibid
[3] "Credit cards are getting smarter" by Anne D'Innocenzio, Associated Press 2001
[4] "The Microchip Miracle-It's already ushered in one revolution— and a second is coming" by Richard J. Dalton Jr., www.future.newsday.com/6/ftop0606.htm
[5] Time Magazine, Article titled "The Big Bank Theory and What it says about The Future of Money" April 27, 1998 Vol. 151 NO. 16
[6] ibid
[7] ibid
[8] ibid
[9] ibid
[10] "Concern over microchip implants-New Technology getting under people's skin" by Jon E. Dougherty 1999 WorldNetDaily
[11] Article by Terry L. Cook, titled "America's Identity Crisis and Coming National I.D. Chip", worthynews.com/Government/chip.htm

Four: The Snare of Benefits

[1] Smart Business, Crime Section, article "Who Else Might be You?" by Thomas Claburn December 2001/ January 2002 issue, page 30
[2] ibid
[3] Federal Trade Commission, Identity Theft Resource Center, Identico Systems
[4] Revelation 14:9-12
[5] Graham Greenleaf, "The Australian Card: Towards a National Surveillance System", Law Society J., Oct. 1987 at 24, 25.
[6] "The Microchip Miracle-It's already ushered in one revolution— and a second is coming" by Richard J. Dalton Jr., www.future.newsday.com/6/ftop0606.htm
[7] Article by Elaine M. Ramesh called "Time Enough? Consequences of Human Microchip Implantation, www.fplc.edu/risk/vol8/fall/ramesh.htm
[8] ibid
[9] ibid
[10] Article by Terry L. Cook, titled "America's Identity Crisis and Coming National I.D. Chip", www.worthynews.com/Government/chip.htm
[11] Article by Elaine M. Ramesh called "Time Enough? Consequences of Human Microchip Implantation, www.fplc.edu/risk/vol8/fall/ramesh.htm
[12] "The Microchip Miracle-It's already ushered in one revolution— and a second is coming" by Richard J. Dalton Jr., www.future.newsday.com/6/ftop0606.htm
[13] "Convict Chip Idea Stirs Ire" by Colleen Heild, Albuquerque Journal, 1999, Issue No. 244
[14] Article by Elaine M. Ramesh called "Time Enough? Consequences of Human Microchip Implantation, www.fplc.edu/risk/vol8/fall/ramesh.htm

Five: The Declaration of Detriments

[1] Revelation 13:16-17
[2] Daniel 12:4
[3] Revelation 14:9-11
[4] Revelation 13:16-17
[5] Psalm 130:3
[6] Revelation 12:10

[7] Article by Terry L. Cook, titled "America's Identity Crisis and Coming National I.D. Chip"

[8] ibid

[9] ibid

[10] John 12:25

[11] Revelation 14:9-11

[12] Proverbs 18:17 The Living Bible, paraphrased by the author for affect.

[13] Matthew 7:13-14

[14] Revelation 20:4

[15] Matthew 10:39

[16] 2 Chronicles 7:14

[17] Hebrews 10:38

[18] Hebrews 11:13-16

Six: Why Worship a Cow?

[1] Genesis 1:24-25

[2] Genesis 9:3

[3] "Bulls, Bears, Even Cars Are Seen in Taurus" by Von Del Chamberlain, Astro Utah Newsletter, Copyright 1999-2000 The Clark Foundation

[4] Internet Article "The Bestiary Cow-Nourishment and Sacrifice" Copyright 1997 by Suzette Tucker

[5] "Isis in the Greco-Roman World" R.E. Witt, 1981

[6] Internet Article "The Bestiary Cow-Nourishment and Sacrifice" Copyright 1997 by Suzette Tucker

[7] Commentary by Marilyn J. Lunberg, Sources: "Bull" in Harper's Bible Dictionary. Ed. Paul J. Achtemeier, San Francisco: Harper and Row, 1985

[8] Internet Article "In Praise of the Cow" "The Hindu Tradition", edited by Ainslie T. Embree. pgs.4-65, Copyright 1966, Random House Inc.

[9] J.C. Hesterman, Encylopedia of Religion, vol.5

[10] Internet Article "The Bestiary Cow-Nourishment and Sacrifice" Copyright 1997 by Suzette Tucker

[11] Internet Article "In Praise of the Cow" "The Hindu Tradition", edited by Ainslie T. Embree. pgs.4-65, Copyright 1966, Random House Inc.

[12] Romans 1:25

Six Continued: Why Worship a Cow?

[13] "Manners and Customs of the Bible" by James M. Freeman, Logos International 1972

[14] Deuteronomy 32:5-6 KJV

[15] Revelation 19:20

[16] Job 31:7

[17] Genesis 13:2 KJV and Job 1:3

[18] Numbers 31:9, 32-33

[19] The New Bible Dictionary, Eerdmans Publishing, Copyright 1962 Intervarsity Fellowship pg. 141

[20] Luke 15:23

[21] The New Bible Dictionary, Eerdmans Publishing, Copyright 1962 Intervarsity Fellowship pg. 202

[22] Exodus 9:1-7

[23] Deuteronomy 25:13-16

[24] The New Bible Dictionary, Eerdmans Publishing, Copyright 1962 Intervarsity Fellowship pg. 1319

[25] Genesis 41:14-36

[26] Article "Weird Cow Facts" angelfire.com 9-20-01

[27] The Learning Network Inc. Article "Cattle" Copyright 2000-2001

[28] "Manners and Customs of the Bible" by James M. Freeman, Logos International 1972 #184 "Baal"

[29] The Zondervan Pictorial Bible Dictionary, Zondervan Publishing House Copyright 1967, pg. 141 Article "Calf Worship"

[30] Numbers 21:33-35

[31] Deuteronomy 3:11

[32] Numbers 32:1-5

[33] Psalm 135:11 // Psalm 136:20-22

[34] The Zondervan Pictorial Bible Dictionary, Zondervan Publishing House Copyright 1967, pg. 42, comments on Psalm 22:12

[35] Amos 4:1

[36] 2 Thessalonians 2:4

[37] 1 Corinthians 3:16

Seven: The Golden Calf

[1] Deuteronomy 7:6-8

[2] First Corinthians 10:11

[3] Acts 7:37

[4] 2 Peter 3:3-4

[5] "Manners and Customs of the Bible" by James M. Freeman, Logos International 1972 #137 "Metallic Idols"
[6] Genesis 46:32-34 // 47:3,6
[7] Romans 1:25
[8] Deuteronomy 8:11-14, 17-18
[9] 1 Samuel 16:7
[10] Matthew 23:25-26, 28
[11] 2 Timothy 3:1-2, 4-5
[12] Matthew 16:25-26
[13] "Manners and Customs of the Bible" by James M. Freeman, Logos International 1972 #138 "Calf Worship"
[14] Times Square Church: Pulpit Series "Seven Thousand Did Not Bow" by David Wilkerson
[15] Matthew 7:21-23
[16] 1 Peter 4:1-4
[17] Exodus 32:33
[18] "Manners and Customs of the Bible" by James M. Freeman, Logos International 1972 #163 "Molech"
[19] Jeremiah 32:34-35
[20] Romans 1:25-27
[21] Leviticus 18:22-25
[22] Romans 6:16
[23] Deuteronomy 29:19-20
[24] Revelation 14:9-12
[25] Psalm 106:19-23
[26] 2 Peter 3:9
[27] Psalm 139:14-18

Eight: Solomon's Double Life
[1] Genesis 1:11
[2] Galatians 6:7-8
[3] 2 Chronicles 7:1
[4] 2 Chronicles 7:12-14
[5] 2 Chronicles 7:19-20
[6] Luke 12:48
[7] Deuteronomy 17:14-17
[8] 1Kings 11:1-12
[9] Nehemiah 13:26-27
[10] 1 Kings 10:28
[11] 1 Kings 4:26

Eight Continued: Solomon's Double Life

[12] Psalm 20:7
[13] Psalm 33:16-17
[14] 1 Samuel 16:7
[15] [199] 2 Chronicles 9:13, 20, 27
[16] 1 Kings 10:18-20
[17] Revelation 1:6
[18] Deuteronomy 17:18-20
[19] John 3:16
[20] Psalm 103:2, 4-5
[21] Acts 10:34 KJV
[22] Romans 2:28-29
[23] Romans 9:6-7
[24] Romans 10:13
[25] John 14:23
[26] Ecclesiastes 1:17
[27] Ecclesiastes 2:8, 10-11
[28] Proverbs 31:4-5
[29] Hebrews 10:23-27
[30] Matthew 12:35-36
[31] Ecclesiastes 12:13-14
[32] 2 Chronicles 7:14

Nine: The Divided Kingdom

[1] 1 Kings 11:11-13
[2] 1 Kings 12:28
[3] 1 Kings 11:31
[4] Revelation 17:17
[5] Revelation 3:10
[7] Who's Who in The Bible, copyright 1994 The Reader's Digest Association Inc. pg. 200
[8] ibid pg. 199 and pg. 369
[9] 1 Kings 12:32-33
[10] 2 Timothy 3:1-5
[11] 2 Chronicles 11:13-16
[12] 1 Kings 12:28
[13] Malachi 1:13
[14] 1 Corinthians 1:18
[15] 1 Kings 12:27
[16] John 1:29

[17] The Seven Festivals of The Messiah by Edward Chumney, ©1994, Destiny Image Publishers pg. 72

[18] Acts 1:8 NU-Text

[19] Romans 14:17

[20] John 14:22

[21] Matthew 6:31-34

[22] 1 Kings 12: 29-30

[23] Exodus 20:3-4 KJV

[24] John 4:23-24

[25] The New Strong's Exhaustive Concordance of the Bible, copyright 1990 by Thomas Nelson Publishers

[26] ibid

[27] "Manners and Customs of the Bible" by James M. Freeman, Logos International 1972 #873 The Mark

[28] Revelation 3:12

[29] 1Kings 12:31-33

[30] The New Strong's Exhaustive Concordance of the Bible, copyright 1990 by Thomas Nelson Publishers

[31] ibid

[32] Genesis 28:13-15

[33] Genesis 28:16-19

[34] Genesis 28:20-22

[35] 2 Chronicles 12: 1-2, 9

[36] James 1:22, 25 NIV

[37] 1 Kings 15:34

Ten: The Covetous Spirit

[1] 1 Thessalonians 5:3

[2] Revelation 14:9-12

[3] 1 Corinthians 6:9-10

[4] The New Strong's Exhaustive Concordance of the Bible, copyright 1990 by Thomas Nelson Publishers, Greek section #4132 #4130 #4123 #4124

[5] Nave's Topical Bible by Orville J. Nave, copyright 1974 by The Moody Bible Institute, pg 250

[6] 1 Corinthians 12:31

[7] 2 Peter 2:12, 15-16, 19

[8] "Manners and Customs of the Bible" by James M. Freeman, Logos International 1972 #688 The Temple Market

Ten Continued: The Covetous Spirit
[9] The New Bible Dictionary, Eerdmans Publishing, Copyright 1962
Intervarsity Fellowship pg. 841
[10] John 2:16
[11] Matthew 21:13
[12] Quran-Surah 2:51 The Cow

Eleven: What Remains is More Glorious!
[1] 2 Corinthians 3:11
[2] Exodus 33:3
[3] Exodus 33:15-16
[4] Exodus 33:21-23
[5] Exodus 33: 19'
[6] Exodus 34:5-7
[7] Exodus 34:10
[8] Exodus 32:9-14
[9] Exodus 34:28
[10] Numbers 11:4-6
[11] Numbers 13:31-33 // 14:3-4
[12] Numbers 14:15-16
[13] Numbers 14:17-19
[14] Numbers 14:20-21
[15] Numbers 14:21
[16] 1 Corinthians 10:11
[17] 2 Corinthians 3:11
[18] Haggai 2:5-9

Twelve: Dominion Like Jesus
[1] 1 Chronicles 12:32
[2] Genesis 2:26-27
[3] John 6:15
[4] Luke 4: 5-8
[5] John 18:33-38
[6] John 3:16
[7] Revelation 13:7
[8] Revelation 12:10-11
[9] John 10:10
[10] Ecclesiastes 3:12
[11] Philippians 4:11-13
[12] 1 Corinthians 6:12-13

[13] Romans 14:20
[14] 2 Corinthians 12:9-10
[15] Luke 19:11
[16] Matthew 16:21-23
[17] Luke 9:44-45
[18] Matthew 20:22
[19] Luke 24:25-26
[20] Philippians 3:10-15
[21] Hebrews 12:1-2
[22] James 5:10-11

Thirteen: What Should Christians Do?
[1] Mark 8:35
[2] 2 Peter 1:3-4
[3] Genesis 2:2-3
[4] Revelation 13:8
[5] Romans 8:31-32
[6] Genesis 5:1-2
[7] Psalm 85:10
[8] Genesis 2:15-16
[9] 1 John 2:15-17
[10] Ecclesiastes 5:10
[11] Revelation 3:17-18
[12] Ephesians 6:6-8
[13] Hosea 4:6
[14] Psalm 106:19-23
[15] Nehemiah 9:18-21

Fourteen: Our Joseph-Jesus Provider!
[1] 1Corinthians 10:11
[2] Hebrews 1:1-3
[3] Genesis 47:14-26
[4] Genesis 37:2-4
[5] Genesis 37:5-8
[6] Matthew 6:11
[7] Genesis 37:9
[8] Philippians 2:9-11
[9] Genesis 41:18-32
[10] Proverbs 13:22
[11] Genesis 42:21-23

Fourteen Continued: Our Joseph-Jesus Provider!

[12] Genesis 45:7
[13] Genesis 42:28
[14] Genesis 45:26-27
[15] Genesis 45:5
[16] Hebrews 13:5-6
[17] Genesis 45:10-11,18
[18] Mark 8:34-38
[19] Genesis 46:4
[20] Hebrews 10:38
[21] Genesis 50:20-21

Fifteen: Don't Give Me Your Bull! - God

[1] Revelation 13:8
[2] Genesis 4:9
[3] Isaiah 1:11-12
[4] Psalm 51:10, 12, 16-17
[5] John 1:29
[6] Hebrews 13:15
[7] Ephesians 1:3
[8] Matthew 23:28
[9] 1Timothy 6:3-5
[10] Mark 9:41
[11] Revelation 14:11
[12] Exodus 32:21-25
[13] 2Timothy 4:3-5
[14] Matthew 5:45
[15] John 3:16

Sixteen: The Last Golden Calf

[1] Hitachi Corporation, WRAL-TV Tom Lawrence Technology Reporter
[2] 1Timothy 6:10 KJV
[3] Revelation 2:13-14
[4] The Zondervan Pictorial Bible Dictionary, Copyright 1963, Zondervan Publishing House, pg.636-637
[5] The New Bible Dictionary, Copyright 1962, Intervarsity Fellowship, pg. 968
[6] The Zondervan Pictorial Bible Dictionary, Copyright 1963, Zondervan Publishing House, pg.636-637

[7] Romans 1:22-25
[8] Isaiah 40:17, 19-20
[9] 2 Thessalonians 2:9-12
[10] 2 Chronicles 7:14
[11] John 14:29
[12] Revelation 1:1
[13] Revelation 3:10
[14] Revelation 13:7, 16-17
[15] Revelation 14:9-12
[16] Jeremiah 17:9-11
[17] James 5:7-8

Order Form

To order additional copies of *The Last Golden Calf: The Microchip Identity*, please use the order form.

Name_____

Address _____

City _____State_____ Zip_____

E-Mail _____

Phone (optional) (   )_____

_____ Copies @ $14.99 US each .... $_____

Shipping ($3.00 first book, $1.00 add. book) $_____

Total..... $_____

Make check or money order payable to:
Henry Vandergriff / Author and send to Lamb Publishing, 11000 Leesville Road, Raleigh, NC 27613

The Author

Henry Vandergriff graduated in 1975 with a Bachelor's degree in Marketing and a Major in Business from Virginia Tech. Henry has been married to his lovely wife Linda, since 1977, with whom he has six children.

He served eight years as an executive account representative before founding Lamb's Christian Center in Raleigh, NC, in 1983, where he still serves as Pastor. His ordination is recognized by Calvary Ministries International (CMI), founded by Bishop Paul Paino in Fort Wayne, Indiana.

The author has been following the development of the "mark of the beast" since 1973. He has interviewed Joseph Woodland, the inventor of the UPC (Bar Code) for IBM and also a patent holder, who wishes to remain anonymous, of microchips for pet and human implantation from the Illinois Institute of Technology.

Henry has appeared on Fox News (nationally syndicated), CBN, the Miracle Network in Canada, numerous Christian TV Networks and interviewed on National Public Radio and talk show air waves across North America.

He has also written, *Mystery Babylon: The Coming Microchip Economy.*